THERE
AND
BACK AGAIN

RESTORING THE CROMFORD CANAL
1968-1988

SIMON STOKER

AMBERLEY

For Hilary, David,
George and my father.

First published 2008

Amberley Publishing Plc
Cirencester Road, Chalford,
Stroud, Gloucestershire, GL6 8PE

www.amberley-books.com

Copyright © Simon Stoker 2008

The right of Simon Stoker to be identified as the Author
of this work has been asserted in accordance with the
Copyrights, Designs and Patents Act 1988.

British Library Cataloguing in Publication Data.
A catalogue record for this book is available from the British Library.

ISBN 978 1 84868 153 8
Typesetting and Origination by Amberley Publishing
Printed in Great Britain

Contents

Acknowledgements

Over the years a great many people, some no longer with us, gave their time, energy and often money in pursuing the dreams of restoring a beam engine, a canal and of operating horse-drawn boats.

Their part in the story must surely be recognised with gratitude.

As must Pat, John and Dougal, without whose example and leadership I would never have had the courage to be a part of the team.

Particular thanks are due to Hugh Potter whose friendship, advice and encouragement over many years has been much valued.

Some of the early photographs are from my father's transparencies (now in my archives) and are marked ADS. Unless otherwise credited all other photographs which appear in this book are my own.

Origins

There is no word in the whole of the English language which so completely and satisfyingly expresses the motion of a canal boat as "glide".

First the patient horse, with the peculiar walk of these animals, passes by with a big belt of gaily coloured bobbins rubbing his side. Then some minutes later the stem of the barge approaches. The boat creeps by without a sound, foot by foot, yard by yard. No haste. No frantic buffeting of the water. No tumultuous wake. It is like a ghost. There is no sound except perhaps the sigh of the rushes or the creak of the rudder. In these days of the motor car one can derive great pleasure and tranquility from the movement of a boat like this.

A. D. Stoker "The Wanderings of the Hebe", 1928

This description of a working horse-boat was written by my father on one of his family's regular journeys around the English canal system in a sail-powered sculling skiff. On this occasion he records the boat "Arcturus" on the Welsh Canal.

No surprise, then, that four decades later he would be one of the leading lights in re-creating horse-drawn boat trips on the Cromford Canal.

Desmond Stoker (*Left*) with my Grandfather, Stephen, (*Centre*) and friend. The skiff, *Hebe* is moored lower right. This picture may well have been taken on the Macclesfield Canal as the boat was kept at High Lane.

ADS

Canal holidays were a regular part of life in my father's family as they had been in my grandfather's. In 1959 we were supposed to be going to Chester but in those days the Trent & Mersey was badly weeded up. The battle between the weak engine and 11″ propeller on my father's first narrowboat – a converted butty named *Stoke* – and the badly maintained canal was one-sided.

We were rescued near Swarkstone by one Tom Lakin and his horse, "Blossom", both of whom used to work the canal. They pulled us back to Shardlow (*above*) and we went somewhere less weedy instead. The man on the cabin roof is my uncle. The boy is me.

A Brief History

The Cromford Canal's history has been covered by a number of authors – particularly in the papers of Prof. R. B. Schofield of Ulster University, Hadfield and Skempton's excellent biography of its engineer, William Jessop, and more recently in photographic form in Hugh Potter's *The Cromford Canal*.

The purpose of this book is not to record the minutiae of historical data but to give an illustration of what happened when a group of enthusiasts went about restoring the upper sections of the canal – the 5 miles between Cromford and Ambergate. However, it is worth recording a brief history in order to put all that into context.

A large area of the Midlands had already been opened up to water transport with the creation of the Trent & Mersey Canal in 1777. Two years later the Erewash Canal was in operation, running from the Trent to Langley Mill, and the possibility of extending further north towards – eventually to Manchester – was enticing. The first stage of that would be the construction of the Cromford Canal, joining the Erewash at Langley Mill and pushing up through the Erewash valley to Ironville. Thence it would cross into the valley of the Amber through the Butterley Tunnel and subsequently turn north again to Cromford on reaching the Derwent valley, a distance of fourteen and a half miles.

The canal received its Act in 1789 and its engineers, William Jessop and Benjamin Outram, were appointed by the Proprietors.

To achieve all this work required – among other things – the construction of the 3,000 yard Butterley Tunnel, two major aqueducts (Bull Bridge and Leawood), fourteen broad locks between Langley Mill and Ironville, three smaller tunnels and, including the Pinxton branch, more than sixty bridges. There are no locks after Ironville and so the canal follows the contour through Butterley tunnel and on to Cromford at about 267 feet above sea level – a major feat of engineering requiring a number of precarious embankments.

The main source of water would be a problem. One of the original plans was to terminate the canal near Cromford Bridge (on what is now Cromford Meadows) and take water via a channel from Arkwright's weir at Masson Mill. (Where Arkwright would raise the weir's height and charge the Canal Company accordingly, ignoring the extra head it would give his mill.) The Canal Company baulked at the cost and eventually decided to place the terminus where it is today (again at the cost of £1,000 in the purchase of extra land from Arkwright) in order to take water from the Cromford Sough via a short connecting tunnel. Even this was not assured as Arkwright diverted the Cromford Sough to provide power in his adjacent mill. A compromise was arranged whereby water not required by the mill at nights and weekends could be diverted into the canal. It is this arrangement which still exists and, as will be illustrated later, can still be a problem! The horseshoe weir in the mill is still visible.

Even from the beginning there was distrust of "the Knight" as he was called by some of his fellow Proprietors. Hardly surprising when John Gell, one of the major shareholders, could say of him:

"Sir Richard has never paid any subscription money. . ." and later *". . .I am convinced he has many designs which the world cannot know of. He has not so much of the milk of human kindness in him as the world would give him credit for."*[1]

A further solution to the supply problem was provided by the construction of the Butterley reservoir which was as much for the use of the Nottingham Canal as for the Cromford.

There is some confusion over the actual date of full operation because of major problems with Jessop's aqueduct at Leawood (a.k.a. Wigwell). Some sources quote 1792 as the year, some quote 1795 since the aqueduct was closed for some time for repairs. In any event the final accounts of 1792 show the canal cost a little over £83,000[2] (something over £8,000,000 in 2007).

It proved highly profitable. From 1802 onwards the Company paid a dividend of 6%, rising to an astonishing 28% in 1840. By 1841-2 goods traffic had risen to 320,000 tons a year. Contrary to received history there is little evidence of the canal being used to carry cotton – most of the tonnage was in lead, iron, coal, stone and similar goods.

Nathaniel Wheatcroft ran a passenger service from Cromford to Nottingham, fares for the 38 mile journey being 4/- first class and 2/- second class (£14 or £7 today).

Water problems returned when the new Meerbrook Sough near Whatstandwell was driven at a deeper level than the Cromford Sough, consequently lowering the water table and depleting the supply. The eventual solution in 1849 was to build a pumping engine next to the aqueduct at Leawood to pump water up from the Derwent 30ft below.

By the 1850's the coming of the far more efficient railways caused the canal company major problems. Tolls were progressively reduced to fight the competition but to little avail. Eventually the directors bowed to the inevitable and arranged the sale of the Cromford Canal to the nearby Manchester, Buxton, Matlock and Midland Joint Railway in 1852. This later became Midland Railway.

The Butterley Tunnel, having suffered repeated closure due to mining subsidence, finally collapsed in July 1900 and the upper part of the canal was isolated. Local traffic continued for some years until abandonment in 1944. The Bull Bridge aqueduct was destroyed in 1968 by road widening and later the construction of the Ambergate Gas Works truncated the canal at the point seen today.

A little over 5 miles of canal remained between Cromford and Ambergate.

1. Schofield: *The Promotion of the Cromford Canal Act of 1789.*
2. Schofield: *The Design and Construction of the Cromford Canal.*

A

BILL

Authorizing the Sale of the Cromford Canal, and other Property of the Cromford Canal Company.

Whereas, an Act was passed in the twenty ninth year of the reign of His Majesty King George the Third, intituled " An Act for making and maintaining a navigable Canal from or from near to Cromford Bridge, in the County of Derby, to join and communicate with the Erewash Canal, at or near Langley Bridge ; and also a collateral cut from the intended Canal at or near Codnor Park Mill, to or near Pinxton Mill, in the said County," and certain persons were thereby incorporated by the name of the Cromford Canal Company, and were authorized to construct and maintain the said Canal, and collateral cut and other works : And another Act was passed in the thirtieth year of the reign of His Majesty King George the Third, intituled an Act to alter and amend an Act passed in the last Session of Parliament for making and maintaining a navigable Canal from or from near to Cromford Bridge, in the County of Derby, to join and communicate with the Erewash Canal at or near Langley Bridge, and also a collateral cut from the said intended Canal at or near Codnor Park Mill, to or near Pinxton Mill, in the said County," and another Act was passed in the Session of Parliament held in the eighth and ninth years of the reign of Her present Majesty, intituled " an Act

The 1846 Bill to sell the canal.

The Birth of Restoration

The canal was disused by the second World war and remained untouched for many years thereafter. Ownership had passed from the Midland Railway Co. via the British Transport Commission to the British Waterways Board. Derelict it may have been but it was still a water channel and even then required basic maintenance. It is difficult to kill a canal!

By the late 1960's a group of enthusiasts were considering restoring the beam engine at Leawood. It was part of the canal property and the group hoped to interest Derbyshire County Council (DCC) in assisting with its restoration.

Eventually it was agreed that DCC would acquire the whole canal between Cromford and Ambergate *as well as* the beam engine and that the group of enthusiasts would form a properly constituted society in order to do the work. Thus was born the Cromford Canal Society (CCS) which was registered as a Charity in 1971.

```
BRITISH WATERWAYS                    P.O. Box No. 9 1 Dock Street
BOARD                                Leeds LS1 1HH

                                     Telephone  Leeds 36741
                                     Chairman Sir Frank Price
                                     Gen. Manager D.G. McCance

Your Ref: BM/JW/P. 304Q

Our Ref:  REO/DV/CROM/A/27/CD

                                           14th September, 1971

Clerk of the Derbyshire County Council,
County Offices,
MATLOCK
Derbys. DE4 3AG

Dear Sir,

        Cromford Canal   (Cromford Wharf to Ambergate)
        Proposed Transfer to Derbyshire County  Council

     I would refer to previous correspondence in connection with the
above and my recent telephone conversation with Mr. Shryane of the
County Planning Department from which I understand that the County
Committee concerned have approved the proposed transfer in principle.


     Upon completion of the transfer the Board shall pay unto the
County Council the lump sum of £16,310 and the County Council
shall covenant to carry out the following works:
```

The canal ownership was transferred to DCC, together with the sum of £16,310 (£166,000 in 2007) which would form the basis for funding. Work could start at Leawood almost immediately (even with the production of a lengthy sheet of disclaimers from BWB!) but these two large and slow-moving organisations did not complete the legal formalities until 1974, so work on the canal was restrained to a few towpath working parties.

Even so volunteers gradually cut back the overgrowth on the towpath and were able to start resurfacing. Better access for all.

The Cromford Canal
The 5 miles from Cromford to Ambergate

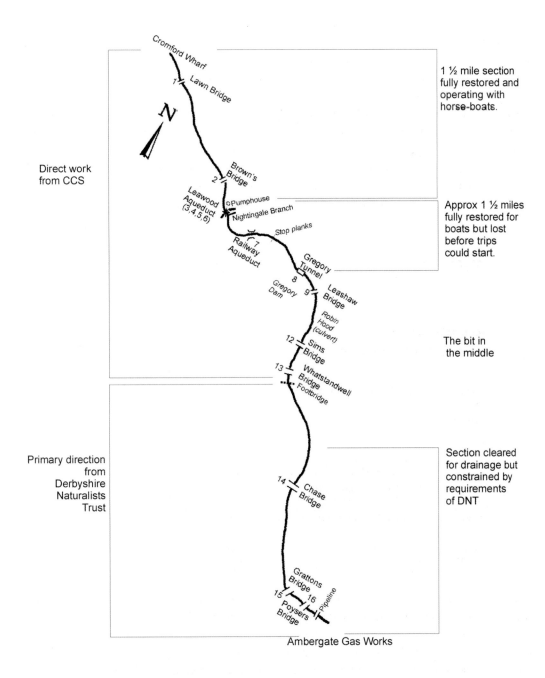

There . . .

Making a start

Where to begin? This is Cromford Wharf *c.*1968. The camera is looking towards the main peninsular part of the wharf – the small warehouse can just be seen in the background – but near-mature trees are not a pretty sight when growing in the stonework. The small, brand new, workboat suddenly appeared when BWB heard of the enthusiasts' group. It was called the 'Lea Wood' and could not have traveled more than 100 yards from Cromford! It disappeared just as suddenly.

A similar sight could be found along most of the length.

(*Above left*) Lawn Bridge (Br 1) was almost totally obscured by tree growth. Reeds by the ground paddle show that the water level was low. (*Above right*) About half way between Cromford and High Peak Junction the canal was shifted sideways to accommodate the new railway and a shunting yard. It came to be known to CCS as 'railway narrows', but at least the reconstruction had left a decent bit of towpath and solid stone walls. Tree growth and silt from land drainage were the main problems here.

Past the railway narrows the canal was filled with slurry. For years silt and tailings from the neighbouring marble-polishing company, Pisanis, had been entering the canal (*above*). For about 150 yards it was almost possible to walk right across the canal on the thick mud. A tiny drainage channel remained, more or less kept open by occasional maintenance.

A few yards on from Pisanis the canal meets the remains of the Cromford and High Peak Railway. Brown's Bridge (Br 2), (*above*) is a swing bridge (which opens on the wrong side of the canal for horses, presumably because of the C&HPR). It had not opened for years and, again, tree growth obscured the structure.

It is adjacent to the bottom of Sheep Pasture Incline (*below*) the first of a number of rope-hauled railway inclines which took the C&HPR over the hills to Whaley Bridge on the Peak Forest Canal, so making the long cherished link towards Manchester.

After Brown's Bridge the canal widens. The (active!) sewage works is below the canal on the left, whilst what is now a broad landscaped path on the right was originally the main line and marshalling area for the C&HPR. In the distance is High Peak Wharf and the original railway height gauge. Further back, on the left, sits the solid building of Leawood Pumphouse.

Even though the canal here is wide, its towpath side on the left is quite shallow, as can be seen from the gentle slope down towards the main channel.

High Peak Wharf in 1974.

This was the transfer wharf from canal to railway. Originally rails ran right through this building so that trucks and/or dry goods could be loaded and unloaded in relative safety. Engines were not allowed!

There is a bit more water in the canal in this picture but the evidence of decay is clear to see.

The heavy reed growth below the canopy was as a result of water run-off from the tracks and also several generations of cinders from railway stoves.

The white post behind the main building is the centre-post of a canal-side crane and is all that remains.

ADS

Just south of High Peak Wharf is the magnificent Leawood Aqueduct (*above*), sometimes called Wigwell, crossing the Derwent in a 80 yard span, with the canal 30 ft above the river.

It gave Jessop major problems during construction – he blamed his use of 'Crich Lime' – and held up full opening of the canal for some time. The tie-bars and other devices used to stabilise the structure are clearly visible on the downstream side. Even after extensive maintenance it still leaked like a sieve, as can be seen from the water marks under the main span.

Upstream on the left bank of the river is a stone facing, which is the intake tunnel for the Leawood Pump. Tucked below the aqueduct on the Cromford side of the river is the large building containing the Leawood Pump (*right*), a beam engine used to pump water up to the canal. The massive stonework is dominated by the building's 95 ft high chimney with its oddly shaped cast-iron cap. In fact the cap is vital to performance as it acts as a venturi to help the draught up the stack. When the boiler(s) are running the draught through an aperture at the chimney base is known to pull in dust and leaves like a vacuum cleaner.

ADS

This area is of such interest that it is worth pausing for a better view.

These two pictures came about because at the time the pumphouse chimney was being inspected by steeplejacks. Very conveniently the Dibnah-style ladders fixed onto the outside had been left in place. It was not a problem for my father to climb the 95 ft up to a scaffolding platform with his Rolliflex. This camera required two hands to operate, so he wrapped an arm round a scaffolding pipe and took these 'aerial' shots of High Peak Wharf and Leawood Aqueduct.

The fixed bridge across the aqueduct (*right*) replaced the original swing bridge (Br 6) and was never in a convenient place. The TA helped us remove it later.

The Nightingale Branch joins the canal at the (far left) end of the aqueduct.

ADS

Both these pictures were taken in a hurry from a light aircraft , hence the grainy quality.

Above left: One of the great 'pinch points' in the English transport network. This is the bend in the Derwent Valley caused by an outcrop (Lea and Holloway) obstructing the natural path of the river. As a result the original track/turnpike/trunk road has to make a broad sweep along the side of the hill below the spring-line. Jessop had to find a way of bringing the canal on its contour on a precarious embankment and then to cross the river by the Leawood Aqueduct. Similarly the engineers of the extra bit of the Cromford and High Peak Railway followed a line more or less level between High Peak Wharf (bottom left) and the new junction with the Manchester, Buxton, Matlock and Midland Joint Railway (top right). From left to right: Railway main line, canal, river, C&HPR link to main line, A6 trunk road (the last three hidden by trees). The flattened area on the bend below the canal contains disused sewage beds. The pumphouse and aqueduct are clearly visible.

On the other hand the adventurous engineers of the MBMMJR dived straight through the outcrop via a tunnel and two bridges, inserting a new aqueduct into the canal where the railway burrowed beneath it. There are few examples in England of three major forms of transport geographically squeezed together like this.

Top Right: Looking down the Derwent Valley from Cromford.

Further down the canal, past the railway aqueduct, the tunnel and just past Robin Hood was the more or less dry section (*right*) towards Whatstandwell. A culverted stream runs under the canal at Robin Hood and at one time the culvert collapsed, causing a big hole in the canal bed. Huge wooden piles had been subsequently been driven into the bed just north of this point which effectively reduced the volume of water coming from Leawood.

In the opposite direction, towards Whatstandwell, the section near Sims Bridge (Br 12) had been dry for a good many years (*right*). This was largely because the iron foundry below the canal and railway complained that the canal leaked into their works, so the paddle was removed, planks inserted at the point where this shot was taken, and the problem was solved in its absence! (When DCC re-puddled this short section the foundry still complained of leaks. A joint CCS/DCC investigation on their site showed the canal culvert blocked with casting sand!) The original Sims Bridge can be seen in the distance. It was rebuilt in steel by DCC later on.

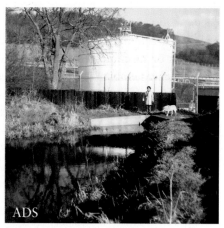

Above left: Another calamity was caused in the early 1970's when Severn Trent wished to drive an interconnecting pipeline from Ogston reservoir to the new Carsington reservoir. A pumping station was established just above the canal (on the right), accessed via Chase Bridge (Br 14). To get the pipeline under the railway and the A6 (both below the canal on the left) STRA cut straight through the canal bed with a dragline machine. This is the result which remained until pressure from local groups via the County Council made them clear up the mess.

Above right: The terminus at Ambergate where East Midlands Gas removed a large chunk of the canal to build its new works.

This picture was taken not long after the works was built – the concrete is still white and the new spillway was not properly protected. These days the whole of this area is thick with trees and vegetation.

Early Work

Before the final transfer of ownership of the canal the main priority was to recover as much as possible of the towpath, especially between Cromford and Leawood.

We were able to promote work parties at weekends, which themselves attracted interest from the public and resulted in a few more members. Of course, no working party would be complete without a source of refreshment (*above right*). Here the motor caravan has been pressed into service as a canteen.

Certainly in those days local companies were much more willing to help out with materials or machinery (and without insisting that a company logo or corporate mission statement was emblazoned for all to see). The large quantities of limestone used here came from local suppliers either at cost or at charitable prices. The dumper truck (*above left*) was also most likely 'borrowed' from a willing donor.

Below left: Lawn Bridge before restoration. The channel is heavily blocked by weed growth. *Below right*: The quality of the towpath was improved considerably from mud to a reasonable surface, gradually extending out from Cromford Wharf.

More towpath clearance (*above left*), this time just above Brown's Bridge near Pisani's. It was quite remarkable how much of an improvement could be made to the appearance of the canal after such work. The youngster, in the image above, had probably bitten off more than he could chew! He is standing more or less in the middle of the canal (roughly top left in the first picture) cutting the reeds so that stronger people might try to clear a drainage channel through towards Leawood.

The blockage was potentially a serious problem as it could cause a build up of water back to Cromford when heavy rain fell.

A similar working party clearing Brown's Bridge (*below*). At least then the structure could be examined.

DCC workmen later made repairs to the woodwork and got it swinging again after many years. Instead of a single pivot point this bridge has a wide cast ballrace with 2″ ball bearings set into a keeper plate. The design was later copied when Br 6 was re-created.

Other early activities included the regular plugging of leaks. This crude, but fairly effective, effort is taking place at the site of the original breach, about 150 yds past the Railway Aqueduct (obscured by the trees behind).

The embankment here is tall and very steep with a top width only just wide enough for a horse. We found signs on the bank sides (to the left) of subsidence and botched repairs. When this section was drained the whole of the nearside part of the channel had been heavily re-puddled in an attempt to stop continuous leakage.

ADS

It may well be that the entire structure was unsound from construction. Ironically this is also the point where the canal overtopped in 1988 – a full breach being avoided because we had installed steel piling along the whole section.

We were fortunate to have the loan of these two Smalley excavators (*below*) from the Waterway Recovery Group. In the foreground is a 'long reach' machine mounted on a rectangular wheeled frame. It worked, but was horribly out of balance when working across its beam as below. The second is a standard 'walking' machine. It was much more stable but had a chronically reduced reach and was really only suitable for tidying up the banks. Someone at WRG tactfully pointed out that they shouldn't really lend them to us at all because the Cromford Canal was no longer connected to the main system. The logic escaped us but apparently it was something to do with their rules. In any case we were certainly grateful for their use, if only to prove that we needed a much more powerful option.

Archive Collection

Big Stuff

The experiments with the little Smalley machines had shown that from an access and a reach point of view they were not at that time suitable for the heavy clearance required on this canal. Fortunately, just at the time when ownership of the canal was finally transferred to Derbyshire County Council, a contact at Shands Engineering told us about a heavy tracked excavator being sold by one of the East Anglia river authorities. This had been converted from a rope (dragline) machine to a hydraulic one and promised plenty of both power and reach to do the job. *"And you can repair it with a hammer. . ."*. So it was arranged that this 9 ton monster, a Smith 14, would be delivered to Cromford. "We'll drive it along the bed of the canal", was the response from one who should have known better! The idea of driving along the bed appealed. The extra reach of the digging arm would allow spoil disposal on both sides of the canal (where permitted) and the theory ran that the flat tracks would most likely help to consolidate the puddle lining.

There being no convenient way into the canal bed at Cromford Wharf the Smith was instead driven across the field from the A6 near Lawn Bridge by a highly apprehensive delivery driver. At the edge of the bank he was urged and cajoled to carry on into the canal, which he did with some misgivings, but lo! the machine did not immediately sink out of sight and remained firm on its tracks. Theory proved to the delight of all parties.

The picture above shows the Smith's first efforts approaching Lawn Bridge. The point of access to the canal is between the two sets of bushes on the upper left bank. This area was easy to work in as the canal bed was firm and spoil could be returned to the field side bank whence it had originated.

ADS

Driving along the bottom is all very well when there is solid ground! From time to time we found 'soft spots'. The Smith learned its first lesson in swimming (*above*) heading towards Cromford Wharf at a point where there seems to be more field than canal. The glutinous soup reached the undercarriage (but not the engine) and successfully prevented forward movement. A local wood yard kindly came with a 'Matador' winch truck and pulled us out. Within 50 yards the bottom was firm again and the machine could travel towards the wharf.

The pictures below show just how much mud there is even after the canal had been drained for some time. *Bottom left:* The feeder arm and winding hole are in the background. Desmond Stoker is clearing the 'air draught'. Health and Safety would have had a field day! *Bottom right:* The dry bottom cleared just outside the winding hole at Cromford.

ADS

ADS

With the canal as clear as possible towards the wharf a corrugated iron (wiggly tin) dam was constructed near Lawn Bridge (*above*). This held a reasonable level of water to keep the channel from drying out but allowed an approach to the rest of the line without the obstruction of the stop planks under Lawn Bridge. It was thought expedient not to return to Lawn Bridge via the canal bottom so the machine was driven through Cromford Meadows and back into the canal near the ground paddle. After that it could clear the bridge hole (*below, left*) and then head for Leawood through silt deltas and reed beds. Once the bridge was cleared the stop planks could be replaced and the tin dam removed.

There was some success in clearing the channel after Lawn Bridge, the bottom was still firm and there was plenty of room to dump spoil (*below, right*). However, 250 yards on, the soft ground returned and the only recourse was to climb out onto the towpath and work from there. The railway sleepers on the towpath side mark the spot where this very large machine made its exit from the channel. This did cause problems; the reach of the digging arm was now severely restricted to a little over half the width of the canal and the towpath was in places too narrow.

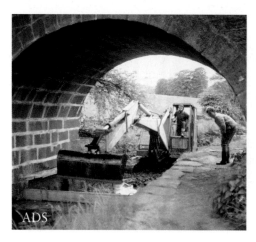

The solution to the narrow path was an ever increasing number of railway sleepers (*above*) which, fortunately, were cheap at the time. Even so, working across the path gave only inches to spare.

At the railway narrows (*below*) there was at least the advantage of a broad and solid platform from which to work. The machine was just able to slew round without hitting the stone wall on the left.

The large coping stones on this section had in many places been disrupted by years of tree growth but the Smith was more than strong enough to lift each stone so that the roots (*right*) could be removed. It is amazing just how much damage can be caused if a little seed is allowed to flourish.

Past railway narrows the canal resumes its original construction. Here there is the first of several trapdoor sluices. Quite why these were built when a standard ground paddle would have been sufficient, is a mystery. They are simple wooden frames with a solid hinged door above and are placed almost in the middle of the channel (*below left*), the gradient of the bed on each side being engineered to allow water to run into them. As a result they are buried under considerable mud and require a strong winch pulling on the attached chain against both mud and water pressure. Once open they are almost impossible to close until the canal is dry.

By late 1975 the Smith 14 was approaching the heavily blocked section by Pisani's works (*below right*). The towpath was again too narrow and railway sleepers were constantly deployed to support the machine. Even so it was only possible to clear a channel little wider than a narrowboat.

The ultimate support! Up to 10 sleepers were used, (*above*) set well down the canal bank, in order to support the machine sufficiently far out so as not to demolish the wall behind. The main line railway runs immediately behind this wall, but 15 ft below! Most of the time this work was done by one or two men (and a dog).

A very clear illustration of how much work was required can be seen below. The camera is at Brown's Bridge looking towards Cromford. On the left is the newly landscaped area, formerly access to train sheds, where the WRG Smalley machines were pictured (p.21) a couple of years earlier.

 With care the Smith was able to access this grassed area, but only to pull mud towards the wharf wall and widen the channel a little more.

These pictures of Brown's Bridge were taken shortly after DCC workmen had made the necessary repairs to get it swinging again. Work to clear the weeds (*above*) was under way. The elm tree on the left (*above right*) was pretty but its roots were a hazard, especially to the bridge abutments (*see* picture p.26). It was felled a few years later.

Two further pictures as clearance continued towards Leawood. Fortunately after the short wall bordering the towpath (*below right*) most of the spoil could be safely dumped down the bank into the old sewage works. The Smith was once again working from the bed of the canal, at least on the gentle slope of the towpath side which was very stable (*below left*). Progress here was much faster than the weeks spent slogging through Pisani's.

By 1977 it was a pleasure to drive the Smith out of the canal at Leawood (via the spillway but don't tell DCC) and rewater the canal. In effect the opening of the canal from Cromford to Leawood – even in rudimentary form – marked the end of the first phase of restoration (but not of the beam engine, whose story is told elsewhere in this book). It allowed us to take stock and consider another of the major objectives: to run a horse-drawn boat on the canal.

A First Boat

By way of a diversion

It was always an aim to operate a horse boat, and by 1975 it was clear that plans should be made. The idea was brought to one CCS meeting, only to be met with a response from one committee member on the lines of "*I think we should have a survey to see if people actually* **want** *a passenger boat. . .*". This classic delaying tactic cost CCS a year in making the decision at a time of high inflation. As a result the cost of the new boat rose from £1,000 to £1,800 (approximately £9,500 today).

Finally the decision was taken and the West Riding Boat Co. Ltd were commissioned to build a 40 ft steel hull to the design shown below.

The boat would be quarter inch plate throughout, instead of the more usual quarter inch bottom with three sixteenths inch sides (even though the sketch above shows otherwise). The Wakefield builders did far more than expected, incorporating little bits of design here and there for the love of it. Being an open boat extra ribs were incorporated for strength as no anti-spread devices could be used as they would be in working narrowboats.

We made a visit to the Wakefield boatyard to see how things were progressing.

Above: Sections of unattached steel plate – not the most attractive things but we were assured that all was going well. To see the front end (*above right*) with *Small Northwich* chalked on the steel was most encouraging!

In the above right image, Alan Hyde is discussing things with one of the builders. (Alan's company was Robert Hyde & Sons, Chesterfield, iron founders. He was also Vice-Chairman of CCS.)

The *Small Northwich* was duly delivered to Cromford Wharf where she spent most of the winter tucked inside the small warehouse behind the crane.

By mid-1977 the line to Leawood was clear and the canal rewatered. The *Small Northwich* was put on the water, her floor filled with tarmac as ballast (which was later found unnecessary and removed) and given a decent coat of paint.

The problem remained what to call her? It was decided unanimously that she should be called *John Gray* in memory of our good friend who had been of immense help in restoring the beam engine (*see* later sections). John was actually a retired surgeon from Sheffield but was also a gifted engineer who did much to encourage many of us to continue the work. He was a man one could respect.

After initial trials CCS started running weekend boat trips and there was immediate interest from the public. At that time in England there were only two or three horse boats running trips, and in Derbyshire the experience was unique. Trips continued for the rest of that season. A regular weekend service was instituted in 1978. At the same time there was increasing interest for private charter trips from a wide variety of groups and schools who realised the value of such things as part of children's education. That year passenger numbers reached 8,000.

By the end of 1978 it became clear that the demand for boat trips (and visits to the pumphouse) could only be met by becoming a full-time organisation. Accordingly CCS became a Company Limited by Guarantee – non-profitmaking, non-shareholding – on 4 January 1979. Arrangements were made with Derbyshire County Council to operate in

this way and to occupy premises at Cromford Wharf. The first full-time employee was appointed later that month, and by February a Job Creation Team had been organised to carry out a backlog of maintenance and to continue restoration.

Above: One of the early trips arriving outside Leawood Pumphouse. At this point *John Gray* was still only 40 ft long and the elaborate side-panels on the cabin had yet to be painted. The horse is called "Major".

One of the early problems of running trips related to the still very narrow channel at Pisani's. The digger had been able to create just enough width to navigate, but for 100 yds getting the boat through was like trying to push a cork back into a bottle. This problem remained for a few more years.

40 ft of boat was clearly not going to be enough! After 1½ years of operation *John Gray* was taken to Shands works at Rowsley in January 1979 where she was cut into two (*above*) and a further 10 ft was added. She returned to Cromford (*below*) to be relaunched at 50 ft.

At around this time an odd situation appeared in the shape of the Board of Trade. It seemed we needed a BoT licence to carry passengers, something we had not imagined before. Apparently in the eyes of the BoT there was no difference between our little horse-boat running on a bit of canal and the QE2 making world cruises!

Accordingly we should carry sufficient lifebelts (presumably for those who could not stand up and walk out of the canal) and other safety gear. The crankshaft in the engine should be examined and possibly changed every year. Tell that to your horse!

To try to iron things out, a visit was arranged by the nearest inspector at a cost of £14 per hour plus VAT from the time he left Hull to the time he returned. Fortunately, on meeting our Chairman, it turned out that they had both been in the same bit of the war. The eminently sensible inspector realised the stupidity of the situation and suggested that, as we had no opportunity to put to sea, the regulations might not be applicable. This was sufficient to keep on operating.

By 1982 demand for boat trips had increased so much that *John Gray* was again taken to Shands and lengthened to 60 ft (her final length). Such was the integrity of the original design that even with an extra 20 ft inserted the hull was as strong as ever. In the picture (*above*) she is in Shands on her side – it was much easier to paint her bottom that way!

In transporting the boat back to Cromford the combined length of boat and lorry was 75 ft – a factor which required a police escort. This was fine until we reached Matlock where the tight roundabout in Crown Square had to be negotiated the wrong way round. Helpful police stopped all traffic and the lorry had to have a burly policeman walking down the middle the narrow and busy Dale Road to move other vehicles, rather like a return of the Red Flag Act (*below*). In this way the *John Gray* became the fastest narrowboat down the A6!

Such a long vehicle had no chance of turning into the narrow wharf entrance and so access was gained via a difficult turn into Cromford Meadows and thence to the waiting crane. She was re-launched straight away (*above*).

In these pictures the new section is clearly shown in the middle, either by the different colour protective paint (*above*) or by the new seating (*above right*).

All the boats (and many other things) had to be chained and padlocked due to constant vandalism or interference. This was annoying and inconvenient and a sad reflection on modern society.

ADS

In 1981 my father decided to bring his boat, *Marjorie A* to Cromford. She was originally a motor pleasure boat (his fourth after three narrowboats) but with his increasing commitment to the Cromford Canal and an understandable lack of crews she was doing very little. We brought her from Swarkstone via the Trent to be lifted out at Langley Mill on the Erewash Canal. From there she was transported by road to Cromford. The engine and living accommodation were removed and the interior converted for passengers, then she was used for a while as an extra or alternative (roofed) boat for passenger trips. It was not unusual to see both boats working at busy weekends. *Above*: *John Gray* and *Marjorie A* together at Cromford Wharf. After a few years she was sold to be restored in the basin at Sheffield. *Below*: "Friday", whose tail can be seen in many of the earlier pictures, on the cabin of *John Gray*. (We called our dogs after days of the week. Don't ask.) This picture made an excellent and popular post card.

Part of the problem with the *Marjorie A* was that she was built of marine plywood which required extensive and continuous maintenance and was vulnerable to bumps and sharp objects. This eventually made her unsuitable for horse work and we found another boat sitting in a farmer's yard up in the hills and miles from water. She was about 50 ft long and the purchase was made. The awful "leisure" conversion was removed, a rudder constructed, new upper works built (*right*) which, with a PVC canopy, would protect visitors from bad weather. She ran regular trips with smaller groups and was capable of providing cooked meals on board for evening outings. She was christened *Duchess* at Cromford (*below*) by Her Grace the Duchess of Devonshire.

Typical pictures of *John Gray* at work.

Passing through Lawn Bridge, the towline still entered the grooves in the stonework worn by every boat since 1795. Indeed if photography had been available then this picture would not be substantially different.

The return journey to Cromford having just passed through Brown's Bridge with a full complement of passengers.

Roy Torrington steering *John Gray* near to High Peak wharf. The colourful traditional canal decoration was very much down to Roy and his family. (He would not normally wear a jacket and tie to steer a boat!)

3rd May 1980

John Gray carries the Duke and Duchess of Devonshire back to Cromford (*right*) following the opening of the restored beam engine at Leawood (*see* p.55).

At the same time the Duke was asked to perform the 'official' opening of the canal, which he did by cutting a ribbon across Cromford Wharf. The boat was held steady (*below*) by a dozen or so Boy Scouts. The boat also carries Committee members, Councillors and some key guests.

May 1988. One of the annual "inspection" trips for those County Councillors involved in canal affairs, together with members of the Derbyshire Naturalists Trust (who directed the lower half of the canal). Desmond Stoker is front left, Roy Torrington is steering.

These pictures were taken while passing through the railway narrows. (*See* also p.12)

John Gray, below approaching Lawn Bridge, returning to Cromford, on a typical summer weekend trip. The towpath is in good condition and clearly a favourite for a gentle walk. The channel is clear and the weeds are under control.

Left: Passing through Lawn Bridge on a weekend scheduled trip.

Right: John Gray waiting for return passengers at High Peak Wharf on a sunny summer's day. Desmond Stoker is at the tiller.

Starting on the 'offside' of the canal was actually much easier since the horse initially pulls the boat away from the bank, rather than on to it. It takes a boat length or so to gain sufficient steerage. Note the well used towpath and absence of weeds from the canal.
By 1982 passenger numbers had risen to 15,000 a year. In one season it was estimated that the combined public and private trips measured a distance in excess of 300 miles
over the 1½ mile section between Cromford and Leawood.

Getting On

Having now become a full-time organisation, and with the assistance of the first of a number of Job Creation Teams, work on both maintaining and restoring the canal could gain momentum. Early work in March 1979 included fitting a secondary sill below Lawn Bridge (*below*) as the original was in poor condition.

Similarly it was necessary to construct a new tail-wall at Brown's Bridge (*below*) so that horses could make a continuous passage over the bridge without having to cast off the boat's towline. This would not normally be necessary as the bridge should swing on the opposite side of the canal. Most likely the close proximity of the C&HPR dictated otherwise so the horses had to learn to love Bridge 2!

The feeder at Cromford was also a cause for concern. At some point BWB had fitted a knife-edge weir on the feeder in order to measure how much water was entering the canal from the mill across the road. This was fine (we worked out a set of calculations which could tell us to the nearest 1,000 gallons an hour how much was crossing the gauge), but the extra concrete tended to cause water to back up in the culvert beneath the road – which always contained debris from upstream – and exacerbate the rising damp in some mill buildings, especially as our access to the main sluice in the mill was restricted.

Our solution was to construct this bypass channel (*above*) in 1979 which was designed to relieve pressure on the main feed when water was too abundant. It worked very well when not being vandalised. The weir can be seen in operation above, with the bypass not in use. It is easy to see how water backed up behind it. Opening the bypass made a considerable difference. The concrete weir has now been removed.

Where the feeder enters the main line, at the winding hole, was also a problem. The sill had deteriorated and the walls were not too sound.

Right: A new sill was fitted and the walls made good.

The culvert from the ground paddle at Lawn Bridge (*see* p.12) runs across the field to a small stream in Cromford Meadows. It was clear from the depressions in the grass that it was not in good condition.

Investigations showed a partial collapse in a couple of places. The culvert is a typical construction – a slab at the bottom, two upright slabs, and another across the top. This works well until there is soil movement or root damage, then water can get into the gaps and eventually cause a collapse.

Here (*left*) the culvert has been cleared prior to repair.

The railings surrounding the output pipe from Leawood Pumphouse had rotted and were a danger both to visitors and to towlines. New oak timbers were supplied and the railings reconstructed (*below*) and painted.

The new railings at the pumphouse (*above*). The winding hole opposite also helps to absorb the wash when the pump is in operation. This is High Peak Wharf at its most attractive.

Once essential jobs had been done and the weather started to improve the Job Creation Team was able to continue working south of Leawood. In this image, the Smith 14 is clearing the junction with the Nightingale Branch next to Aqueduct Cottage.

After the work was completed and the canal re-watered.

While working at Aqueduct Cottage we took the opportunity to have a look at the 'stop lock' into the Nightingale Branch. A wide and very solid wall had been built across part of the chamber both to allow access to the cottage and to prevent water getting into the branch line. We were, however, able to uncover the furthest gate position and its sill. From the little evidence discovered it is difficult to make a firm statement on how this 'lock' worked. The most likely explanation is that in fact it consisted of two opposing lock gates which would regulate water levels relative to the branch and the main line. Certainly there is no lock chamber as such, so both gates would have to be opened to allow boat passage through. Excavations of the chamber can be seen above. It is clear after the removal of spoil (*above right*) that there was at least one gate (the indents in the walls) and a stop plank position. The other gate may well have been buried in the barrier wall built across the chamber.

Just round the corner from the end of Leawood Aqueduct is another ground paddle. Like the one at Lawn Bridge this was not draining properly and investigations of the (circular) culvert down to the river showed a blockage immediately behind the sluice and under the towpath. When we dug out the towpath we found a hole of about 4 ft in diameter had been washed out which was 9 ft deep and covered only by a thin crust of towpath surfacing. It could have collapsed at any time! The damage was repaired and, instead of backfilling such a large hole, a chamber was built under the towpath to aid future maintenance (*below*).

Working the Smith along the next section (on the canal bed) was a simple operation. However, a serious obstacle loomed in the shape of the Railway Aqueduct (Br 7). This iron structure was inserted into the canal to allow the passage of the new railway though the hillside of Lea (*see* p.17). A number of people were consulted on whether it would be possible to drive the heavy machine over such an apparently delicate structure. When the mud was cleared (*above*) some serious calculations could be done on its strength. The conclusion was that the interior should be lined with a layer of fine limestone and two layers of railway sleepers (opposing each other to spread load). However, the machine must only be driven across on a Sunday when no trains were running.

The crossing was made on 12 August 1979. British Rail were notified and were in attendance, along with people from DCC. Key members of CCS were also there to watch in case the machine crashed through the iron onto the railway 20 ft below.

The temptation was to move the heavy machine as fast as possible over the aqueduct and hope for the best. Advice was, however, to creep as slowly as possible in order to allow the structure to take the weight properly. The driver was probably more nervous on this exercise than at any other time in the whole restoration of the canal – and with some justification!

12 Aug '79

Styx? Rubicon? Whatever it was we crossed it without incident.

Then on to the long section which had breached in 1920 (*Below*).

About 300 yards from the Railway Aqueduct the long straight ends in a sharp-ish corner, turning the canal towards Gregory Tunnel.

Fortuitously, in view of the repeated problems on this section, a stop plank position had been built roughly half way between aqueduct and tunnel. We never found a name for it and it is not mentioned on the maps or in the 1908 edition of Bradshaw's (de Sallis). However, there is a sort of 'bridge' marked on the 1811 canal map, although when we cleared the site no clear evidence of a bridge was found. For want of a description it was christened 'Gregory Nip'. Here two of the workforce are inserting new stop planks.

Working along the bottom on this section was reasonably satisfactory. We passed Gregory Nip and moved on towards the tunnel. However, after the next corner the canal appeared virtually bottomless! The embankment here is extremely narrow – not even wide enough to take a dumper truck in safety (the towpath had to be widened in many places) – so the stark choice was either to return to Leawood by the way we had come or somehow to swim the lumbering machine through the liquid mud for 150 yards to the tunnel (*below*). Inspiration was provided by no less than George Stephenson, who 'floated', the Liverpool and Manchester Railway across the great bog known as Chat Moss in 1829. Could we float our machine in the same way?

At least we had two advantages: the offside of the canal was covered in dense brushwood (mainly silver birch) which would have to be cut back anyway, and we had a pretty good supply of railway sleepers. Stephenson's technique was essentially to float a raft of logs and brushwood on which to build his embankment. We used the same idea.

One group cut the brushwood from the canal side and laid a sort of web with it just ahead of the digger. A second group laid two layers of sleepers across this web. The sleeper mats were at right angles to each other and so spread the weight of the machine across what became a raft. Then the heavy Smith would inch carefully forward on top of the sleepers and just as carefully do what work was possible. It was like working on top of a vast and stinking jelly. Any rash or sudden movement by the machine could have destabilised its position and so all work was taken slowly and carefully. Then the machine would lift the sleepers round to its front for a new raft, dig out the brushwood and dispose of it and the process would start all over again – a machine length at a time (*above*).

The idea is simple enough but to work for weeks in those conditions in foul smelling, clinging, mud where each sleeper became heavier as it became more encrusted with mud was very hard work indeed. Full credit to everyone who was involved in that exercise. These two pictures give a fair idea of the problems involved.

A Smalley 5 Long Reach (*above*) was delivered to Cromford late in 1979. It was much improved on the earlier versions, although still a 'walking' machine which pulled itself along by use of the digging arm. A single-cylinder Lister engine provided just about enough power. Its most important asset was the ability to travel along the towpath, and even though the reach was restricted it was of great use. It was also surprisingly agile. When faced with the low arch of Lawn Bridge it was a fairly simple operation to bypass the problem and get back on to the towpath by climbing the wall (*below*) out of the field. (Keen observers will note a Tirfor winch attached for safety!)

The Long Reach Smalley was especially useful in bankside work. It could get along most of the towpath and clear the weeds (*above* at Pisani's), which the big Smith could not do with a less discriminating bucket. It may have looked like the business end of a preying mantis but it did the job. However, there was still the problem of that lack of reach. . . .

From time to time we were blessed with volunteers willing to give a day's work (or more) just for the sake of it. *Above right*: Army 'volunteers' using their abseiling techniques to defoliate both sides of Leawood Aqueduct. This was a most important job as trees had taken root in the crevices between stones and were happily doing what trees do best – cracking the stonework.

For a civilian organisation to mount such a task would have required considerable scaffolding and safety gear. These lads hung a rope on a Land Rover and got on with it. They did a similar job on both ends of Gregory Tunnel where the stonework was also being attacked by roots. Great stuff!

Some of the other volunteer groups included: Engineering apprentices, Girl Guides, Nurses (in training), Matlock Fire Brigade, Alfreton Young Offenders (under supervision), Scouts, Foreign exchange students and no doubt a number of others. All such help was most gratefully received. As far as can be recalled none of them went abseiling!

Working from original photographs we proposed to DCC that the canopy over the dock by the larger warehouse at Cromford should be rebuilt. Plans were drawn up and materials were provided for the Job Creation Team which did the work. With very slight modifications to the original design the structure was re-created using the original iron stanchions and wall plates (*above*).

The roof was covered with hot-rolled felt by contractors, but it was felt necessary to "age" the appearance. Accordingly hessian sheets were placed on top of the felting and then given a coat of bitumastic paint.

Below: The finished structure. Note also the skeleton of the icebreaker rescued from Leawood which it was intended to preserve on the wharf.

Above: How the wharf looked after completion of the dock canopy.

A serious problem was that water in the main part of the wharf tended to freeze in the winter. (Even though the winding hole did not.) This might not be thought serious except that it invited foolish people to try their luck on the thin ice and thus represented a safety problem. The same water in summer was effectively 'dead' because there was no circulation.

In laying a new electricity cable to the small warehouse we literally unearthed the remains of a substantial culvert which must have been the original feeder to the canal before the drydock extension was built. (This also accounted for the strange shape of the office building.) It was a fairly simple matter to lay a couple of 4″ pipes into the original culvert and feed 'warm' water to the main wharf. The original exit was carefully excavated (*right*). A bonus was that in summer the main wharf contained 'fresh' water which helped to inhibit the growth of green algae and weeds.

In the mid-1980s attention turned to the lower sections of the canal between Whatstandwell and Ambergate. In view of the fact that it was unlikely that regular boat traffic would run on this length, and also because of a potentially higher interest in the local flora and fauna, the main directions came from the Derbyshire Naturalists Trust (DNT). At times the interests of restoration and conservation produced a dichotomy of ideas. On the one hand there would soon be no canal at all if basic restoration could not be carried out, on the other hand the DNT's insistence on preserving

"marginal vegetation" (ie weeds etc.) would be a problem. The big Smith could not get to this section and so another Smalley tracked machine was hired to do what work was possible. At the very least it was necessary to clear a drainage channel over the whole length, otherwise stagnant water would change entirely the nature of whatever life was in the canal. Starting at Whatstandwell (*above*) this machine worked from the bank sides, tipping spoil into dumpers which could transport it to agreed dumping points. It was possible to work steadily along for some time, and removing the cabin of the machine allowed access under the bridges. However, the machine was wider than the available towpath beneath some bridges so the solution was to insert steel beams topped with planks. (*Below* at Grattons Bridge, Br 15.) In this way a channel was cleared all the way to Ambergate and what available water there was could flow to the spillway there.

Leawood Pumphouse

Parallel Emotions

The wonderfully solid buildings at Leawood containing the engine and boilers with its 95 ft chimney. Why it was built to such a grand scale is open to speculation.

The beam engine at Leawood was built in 1849 to provide a lasting solution to continuous water supply problems experienced by the canal company. It has been said that at first a pumping engine was hired by the company, and worked at a point somewhere nearby. No trace of this engine – for example the massive foundations or the bob wall carrying the beam – has been found. It may have been sited on ground now occupied by the next door sewage works. The permanent installation was commissioned from Graham & Co of Elsecar. It is a Cornish-*type* engine, although cannot be described as a true Cornish beam engine as there are significant differences in the operation of its valve gear.

The massive cast iron beam is 33 ft long (31 ft between the connecting rods) and is estimated to weigh about 20 tons. It is driven by a 50 inch steam cylinder with a nominal stroke of nearly 10 ft (giving it a volume of 235,650 cubic inches, or around 3,861,600 cubic centimetres, a little bigger than the average Ford Escort!). It is a single-acting engine. Steam is supplied from two locomotive-type firetube boilers in the adjacent building. (Note: these are not original but ones installed by Midland Railway in March 1900.)

The rocking of the beam actuates a massive plunger pump of similar dimensions to the steam cylinder and operates in much the same way as a valved syringe. As the plunger is extended water is drawn via an access tunnel 150 yards long from the River Derwent and up through the intake valve, and then (there being no return driving stroke) the sheer weight of the plunger (about 15 tons depending on how it is ballasted) forces the water past a second – output – valve and up a 4 ft diameter pipe into the canal. The difference between river and canal is about 30 ft and each stroke of the engine pushes around 3½ tons of water up the pipe. Even the two valves are massive. Each is a cast iron double-beat equilibrium valve – a fixed but open lower part on top of which a bell-shaped upper part is allowed to move a few inches. The bell shape has two working faces which sit upon matching seats in the fixed lower part, the top seat on each valve is about 13ft in circumference and the bottom seat is about 14ft 6ins. Thus large amounts of water can move through and around the valve as the extensive circumference compensates for an opening of only a few inches. Even so, each valve weighs at least 1½ tons. The engine is reputedly capable of pumping at 7 strokes each minute, although to wind it up to that speed requires considerable steam and is positively frightening! A more comfortable speed was found to be around 3 or 4 strokes/min. Even so this pumped about 14 tons of water a minute into the canal – or 840 tons and hour (about 188,000 gallons).

Work to restore the beam engine began in a small way in 1971. The property had not yet been transferred to the ownership of DCC, but we (having signed a lengthy BWB disclaimer) were allowed access to see what was required. The building was indeed in a sorry state. The windows had been boarded up, the place was dripping with damp, limewash was peeling from the walls and just about every mechanical piece was badly rusted. There was no natural light and no electricity.

Left to right:
Alf Etchells
(ex railwayman
from Derby),
Simon Stoker,
John Gray, and
Peter Gray
(John's son).

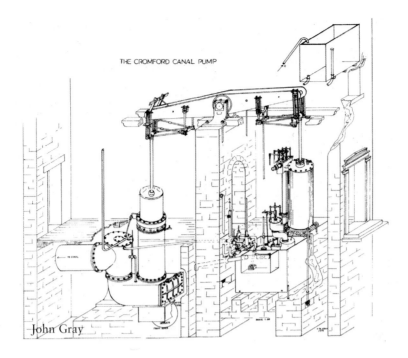

THE CROMFORD CANAL PUMP

John Gray

Finding out how everything worked was a major occupation in the earliest stages of restoration. The basics were fairly obvious, but the way the steam valves worked and in what sequence was something of a mystery, as was the presence of a little device called a dashpot attached to the valve gear. (On a visit to the famous Crofton engines such a device was absent.) Clearly the Watt Separate Condenser was in position but it was below the steam cylinder rather than on the other side of the 'bob' wall (as it would be in a mine engine). The pump itself was covered in many layers of paint and rust and its exact operation was not immediately obvious. There was a 'spare' water valve outside and we could venture down the dry outlet pipe from the canal to look at the upper valve in position. This told us much, but not all.

Above: John Gray's drawing of the engine from 1973. He later acknowledged a couple of errors in it but nevertheless the essentials are correct. The steam cylinder, bob wall and pump unit all have massive foundations which carry their weight more or less independently from the building. John has correctly included the massive tie bolts which hold down the steam cylinder and main trunnions. The condenser unit is below and to the left of the steam cylinder. Amid a jumble of pipes and valves is an additional pump which moves condensate back up to a huge tank set into the roof space above the gallery. From there warm and treated water could be sent back to the boilers. Spare condensate and extra cooling water is exhausted into a space between the bob wall and the pump unit. The engine operates essentially on about 75% vacuum from the condensers and 25% steam pressure from the boilers. It was often fun talking to visiting lovers of internal combustion engines and explaining that on this engine both the input and exhaust valves are open at the same time (they failed to understand). The difference is made by an intermediate valve – the equilibrium valve – which controls passage of steam to the lower part of the cylinder and thence to the condensers.

Interested persons on a visit to the pump. *Left to right*: Simon Stoker, Alan Hyde, Ruth Hyde (behind Alan), ?, John Gray, Andrew Stoker, Sir David Huddie, ?, ?, ?, The Duke of Devonshire. His Grace was extremely keen that the engine should be restored and was most encouraging. (Apologies to those unnamed).

Below: Two pictures of the (steam) valve chest (*left*) at a time when work was just starting, and (*right*) during restoration. In the bottom right picture the input valve is on the left and the equilibrium valve on the right. Originally the whole engine had been painted a rather dull green. It was said that Midland Railway probably had a surfeit of the stuff and sent some up to Cromford to get rid of it.

ADS

Several attempts were made to survey the intake tunnel from the river. In these pictures members of Matlock Sub Aqua club are preparing to enter at the river end. It was found that the river had left a huge sandbank inside the mouth of the tunnel which was impeding water flow. This was removed by squirting it with high pressure hoses, first ineffectually by a TA group whose pump was not adequate (well it wasn't designed for that!) and later very effectively by Matlock Fire Brigade and a portable fire pump (which was!) Divers eventually managed to swim all the way to the pump chamber and surfaced underneath the massive intake valve.

ADS

In 1973-4 DCC started re-roofing the building to make it weatherproof. To preserve its fine lines the original architect/builder had created wide leaded gutters which drained water down a pipe *inside* the building. Lack of maintenance over 40 years had ensured that the gutters had filled with leaves and debris, causing water to spill down the inside walls, rotting the roof trusses in the process. The trusses and other suspect rafters were replaced along with some interior beams and then the Yorkshire slate roof was replaced. The building is Gade 2* Listed so DCC were able to find some grant-aid for these jobs. During this period sunbathing up there was at a premium!

Above: DCC workmen re-roofing. DCC were able in 1973 to obtain a grant of £5,613 (£48,800 today) from the Department of the Environment.

The new trusses and rafters during re-roofing.

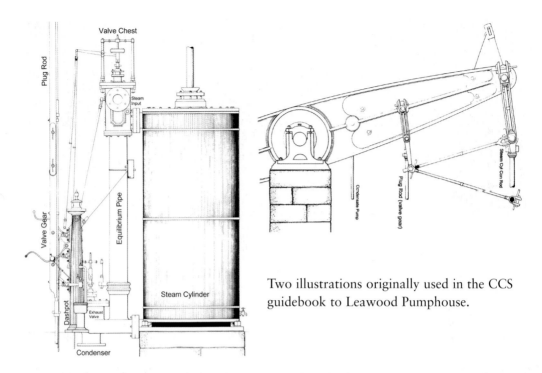

Two illustrations originally used in the CCS guidebook to Leawood Pumphouse.

Above left: A cross-section of the steam cylinder and its associated valve gear. The engine operates by allowing steam into the top of the cylinder which provides some (but by no means all) downward force on the piston. This of course rocks the beam, causing the plug rod to descend. One of two large wooden cams on this rod will contact a valve lever (the lower 'S' shaped one on the left) and cut off the steam at a predetermined point. At a given interval after that the dashpot triggers the release of the equilibrium valve, allowing the steam to be forced out of the cylinder, down the equilibrium pipe and back into the cylinder below the piston. This transfer is cut off hopefully before the piston crashes into the top of the cylinder, leaving a 'steam cushion' to help. The valves re-set and the process starts again, except this time there is exhaust steam under the piston. The opening of the input and exhaust valves simultaneously allows the previous charge of steam to be pushed out into the condenser where cold water considerably reduces its volume, thus providing a healthy vacuum of up to 25″ mercury. It is this vacuum which does most of the pulling on the piston, making the engine much more efficient.

The real difference in this engine is the use of a dashpot. This is an oil-filled cylinder with a piston being pulled through the oil. A little hole in the piston can be adjusted in size to give faster or slower travel. It is this device which controls the 'rest' interval between the full downward (power) stroke and the return (pumping) stroke. In fact a tiny little screwed handle on the device controls an engine two houses wide and three houses high!

Above right: James Watt's other great invention, the Parallel Motion, which keeps the piston rod (and the pump rod at the other end) in a straight line while allowing the end of the beam to describe an arc. This was the vital device which not only removed dangerous ropes or chains but allowed the development of the double-acting beam engine. (That is both pulling *and* pushing.) Watching the motion in action is a joy to behold.

Below the floor in the pump chamber lie the two huge cylinders of the pump unit (*above left*). Nearest to the camera is the plunger cylinder with a massive inspection plate bolted to its lower part. Behind that is the output cylinder containing the upper (output) valve.

Water is sucked up into the rectangular chamber below the plunger through the intake valve and then forced horizontally and upwards past the upper valve into the pipe to the canal. Early inspection showed that the seats on both valves had rotted badly and were thus useless. The only way to get to the bottom valve is through the heavy cast iron inspection plate (weighing a couple of tons) which has to be unbolted and moved out of the way. Then the upper (bell shaped) part of the valve has to be removed *horizontally* as there are only a few inches to spare. Only when this is done can access be gained to the valve seats.

The seats are made of wood, most likely the originals would have been hornbeam. It was necessary to have made individual pieces of tanalised oak about 4″ wide and radius-cut to either top or bottom diameter. These pieces are also tongue and grooved on their sides (like floorboards) and slotted again along their bottom face. They fit into a half-dovetail groove in the casting. The work on the seats of both the huge valves was done almost entirely by John Gray who patiently spent hours and hours in the cramped, dirty and damp conditions. He even manufactured special tools to help the process. Each piece of oak had to be fitted on the groove of its neighbour and a small foxtail wedge inserted in the slot at the bottom. Then it was clamped sideways to prevent a gap forming. Following that the piece would be hammered gently home, the foxtail wedge expanding the base and locking the piece in situ. Over 500 separate operations were required on each valve before the upper bell could be replaced.

Above right: The lower (intake) valve in situ with the inspection plate removed. Just how little space is available is clear to see. The flat circular thing above the valve is the base of the plunger – all 15 tons of it hanging over any work being done!

The brass fittings to boilers number 43 and 44 had been stolen (literally knocked off with a hammer) and so replacements had to be found and modified to fit. In 1975, after four years work on the engine it became possible to raise a little steam (*above left*). The steam cylinder was warmed through and the beam very gently rocked to see how it would react.

Unfortunately this operation caused a large horizontal timber to crack. This timber beam runs right across the building to support the two 'saddle' beams on which the actual cast iron beam rests. At 17 ft long it had been replaced with pine during DCC's work on the building, and whilst this was no doubt correct from a static point of view it was inadequate when one end of the engine depended on it for support. The stroke of an engine such as this can vary (there is no crank to limit travel) and any mis-timing of the valves can cause the pumping end of the engine to hit the saddle beams. In normal operation this does not happen, the engine stops a couple of inches above the saddle, but when the cylinder is cold or the valves do not properly operate bottoming can happen. As a result the engine was stopped and could not work until the pine was replaced.

Above right: The pump plunger partially raised and blocked in that position while work went on below. The square rope on the right is a piece of the gland packing, several rings of which sit below the ring of red bolts (the stuffing ring). The full height of this massive cast iron cylinder can be seen on p.67.

The main gland (*see* later) is effectively the only seal between the plunger and the canal above.

The defective pine timber was replaced by DCC with a 16″ x 12″ Greenheart beam which had to be passed through the pumphouse wall at the correct height for fitting.

At the time the canal was dry (*above left*) so moving this 17 ft timber was achieved by building a scaffolding bridge across the canal.

By 1977 Alan Hyde had completed his calculations on the new Greenheart beam and revealed further problems:-

1 – The original pine was most likely right up to its limit on load carrying, even on a static load.

2 – The new Greenheart beam was 4 times stronger.

3 – Due to this if the engine 'bottomed' again the cast iron would break rather than the timber!

From the beginning of restoration we had noted two tie-bars supporting the saddle beams and were aware that there may well have been similar problems in the past. These tie-bars were attached to an independent oak beam running across the gallery at roof level. Alan's plan, approved by DCC, was to re-attach the tie-bars but with pre-stressed calibrated spring washers. To do this required the removal of the old oak beam and the installation of twin steel joists of the same dimensions. The joists were held slightly apart by welded blocks and the tie-bars could pass between them and be bolted to the top of the beams. This is fairly simple, except that the whole operation had to take place 10 ft above the gallery, which itself was over 20 ft above the ground floor with a clear drop straight down. We built a 'bird cage' of railway sleepers (so useful!) to provide a stable platform (*above right*) on which work could be carried out and then carefully removed the original timber, lowering it down to the ground floor. The two halves of a steel joist were raised the same way and inserted into the original positions.

Following this, Alan arrived with micrometers and, by slightly raising the beam, we could calibrate the deflection on the joists, and thus the spring washers, at 25 tons deflection per inch. It was a complicated and time consuming operation but it worked.

The main gland on the plunger had to be replaced on a regular basis (*above*). This required draining the output pipe and removing the stuffing ring (with the hoops on) to remove the old packing. New packing of 2″ square hemp rope soaked in tallow is then inserted and the stuffing ring replaced. Such is the area covered that the bolts on this ring need only be little more than finger-tight for it to work properly.

Almost from the beginning of our work in 1971 people began to wander in to the building to see what we were doing. By the time the passenger boat started running we were able to give guided tours of the engine, especially on educational visits which often combined boat and pumphouse.

Right: A youngster on a school visit, suitably dusted with coal, is being photographed by a reporter from The *Daily Telegraph.*

After eight years of slow progress we could finally fire the boiler and try a first proper steaming of the engine. Given that the machine had not moved for 40 years there were a few minor teething problems but by May 1980 we were ready to invite the Duke and Duchess of Devonshire to perform an official opening ceremony (*see* also p.38). The engine was restored and operational. It was of huge regret that John Gray had died some years earlier and was not able to see the fruits of his labour.

Above left: Looking through the massive bob wall to the valve gear with the steam cylinder behind. The big pipe to the top right is the steam line entering from the boiler house. The dashpot is the little device at the bottom right of the valve gear.

Above right: The plunger sitting quietly at rest. We added two little gauges to show suction and pressure. The tap below these gauges is vital to remove any air in the cylinder since it is the resistance provided by the water during the pumping (downward) stroke which prevents the plunger crashing through the bottom of the cylinder and taking the rest of the engine with it. The new Greenheart beam can be seen running across the chamber at the top of the stairs, just above and behind the crosshead of the parallel motion. Most of the flooring was replaced by DDC and metal grilles installed so that visitors could see what was happening down in the bowels of the machinery. In operation the engine is nearly silent but the constant swirl and crash of water from the condensers can be frightening to some people!

A mildly amusing event occurred at around this time. We received a telephone call from Severn Trent Water Authority which went something like:-
"We are going to charge you for abstraction of water from the Derwent"
"Oh really?"
"Yes but don't worry, the rate will only be 0.002p per litre" (Or something like that.)
"What's a litre?" (working out at 7p per stroke, 28p a minute or about £67 *a day*.)
"Do you know how much water that pump can shift?"
"No"
"Have you read the Cromford Canal Act?" (Which allows the engine to take water at certain times.)
"No. It doesn't exist".
"Well it does exist. Go and read it and come back to us when you have."
The call was never returned and Severn Trent seemed after that to ignore the situation.

Above left: The restored beam of the engine. This weighs about 20 tons and is made of two flanges of cast iron. The ribs cast on the outer sides are to add strength. Alan Hyde, an iron founder himself, estimated it would take each casting about two weeks to cool to avoid warping before it could be handled. The axle in the centre is 12″ in diameter and is supported by two trunnions with brass bearings. The whole weight of the beam is carried on the massive bob wall running down the middle of the building to its own foundations. In effect the actual 'house' carries little or no load from the engine. In the lower right of the picture is one of the two saddle beams of the pump end of the machine. There are two more at the steam cylinder end. These saddle beams are only fixed at one end – the bolt can be seen – and are slightly sprung at the other end to help take any 'bounce' out of the moving beam should it touch them.

Above right: The huge plunger of the pump at full stroke. It is a magnificent sight. Here the cylinder is glossy after regular work through the main water gland, unlike the picture on p.63. The newly fitted pressure and vacuum gauges are visible on the gland housing.

It is thought this may be the biggest plunger pump remaining in England. There are others but they are generally smaller due to a variety of factors, including the head they have to pump against. Certainly this is the only pump of its type, it being completely visible.

With the engine at full stroke the plunger is fully raised and the steam piston is fully depressed (*right*) in its cylinder.
The input (left) and equilibrium (right) valves are in front of the main cylinder. These too are double-beat valves made of brass.

This picture also gives an excellent example of Watt's Parallel Motion in action – its purpose being to maintain the piston rod in a straight line. This was the major breakthrough which allowed single-acting engines to become double-acting, although as at Leawood it became just as common on single-acting Cornish type engines.

Below: What 3½ tons of water looks like when it reaches the canal on a pumping stroke. We kept the stop planks of the pipe in place (just visible across the output) to reduce surging and just in case one of the water valves did not close properly and drained the canal. (In 2008 this very problem, caused by worn or rotting valve seats, required the output pipe to be drained, unless the pump was in action, otherwise the canal could lose water quickly.)

Archive Collection

LEAWOOD
PUMP
HOUSE

Featured in the
BBC/Open University
Programme –
"Sources of
Power"

Schools Working Day

PROPOSED STEAMING DAY: 20th APRIL 1988

The unique working Beam Engine built in 1849 to pump water into the Cromford Canal.

As an educational tool, there is little substitute for the experience of a visit to a working site.

When it comes to operating beam engines in their proper way the cost of a school visit can be very high.

HOWEVER, the Cromford Canal Society is proposing to establish a special steaming of the engine, especially for school parties, whereby the cost of running the engine can be shared.

To establish a special 'sharing day' will need about 250 visitors in order to reach a projected entry cost of 75p per person.

Already some visiting schools have shown an interest and expressed a wish to be involved. ARE YOU INTERESTED?

Depending on your numbers it will be possible to book an exclusive period in the day when only your school will be admitted. This will give you time to see the engine at work, to ask questions, and talk to our staff.

Remember: We can only share the cost if sufficient demand is shown by our schools visitors.

Contact us with your bookings and questions:

CROMFORD CANAL SOCIETY
OLD WHARF, MILL LANE,
CROMFORD, DERBYS. DE4 3RQ
Tel: Wirksworth (062 982) 3727

CROMFORD CANAL

HISTORY AT WORK

This fine gentleman (*above left*) is unidentified but the photograph is thought to be around 1900 – 1910. With the length of time it took to bring the engine back into working condition it might be expected that there would be more useful photographs. Of course there are, but most are of a technical nature and do not readily identify the engine as a whole. In fact the story of the engine restoration is one of tiny advances, often taken in damp, dark conditions. For instance for the first two or three years we had no electricity to work with – power was provided by a small petrol generator lent to us by DCC. Only later was it arranged that a new electricity supply should be installed, and then largely because DCC was itself developing the Wharf Shed at High Peak as a residential centre. There were really no quantum leaps where we could say "now we go", more a continuous grind of taking a part of the engine, cleaning and restoring, and then moving on to the next part. And it is a big engine! That so many people stayed the course, is in itself an achievement. It is necessary to have considerable faith in the eventual outcome to spend so many hours working in often difficult conditions. It must also be remembered that the work on the engine was going on simultaneously with work on the canal, sometimes sharing the same people. Although a number of the volunteers involved tended to specialise in the engine work, an equal number shared their time with helping on the boat operations or in the souvenir shop. For instance in 1973 the log records work being undertaken from late January to late December with well over 1,500 man-hours. In addition – and this was still before boats were operating – there were 300 school visitors and about 400 casual visitors.

This sort of work cannot be done without considerable goodwill from other people and from local companies. Another note in the 1973 log records valuable contributions from: Matlock Sub Aqua Club; Matlock Fire Service; the TA (Herts); Scouts; Stancliffe School; H. J. Enthoven Ltd; Bryan Donkin Ltd; John Smedley Ltd; Shell, and there certainly were many others.

Getting On Again

Continuous work with various machines since the 1970's had not solved the crucial problem: how to get any kind of machinery to reach right across the canal in order to dredge and to maintain.

By this time a number of small hydraulic machines were becoming available and Smalley Excavators had started to produce floating dredgers based on new designs. Various ideas were considered, including a sort of marsh machine with a huge screw at the front which in theory could move along and vacuum up practically everything. It was not, however, suitable because it cut a flat profile (the canal bottom is rounded) and required miles of piping to carry slurry to a suitably constructed mud pond.

Ultimately, with the help of DCC and the manufacturers, it was decided our Long Reach Smalley 5 could be mounted upon a specially made pontoon and have stabilisers added so that it could float along and dredge just about anywhere. Smalley's standard pontoon was too wide to go through our bridges and feeder arm and so a slightly narrower version was specially built. The undercarriage of the old machine was removed and a more powerful twin cylinder engine (with electric start!!) was substituted. The new machine could not be called one of Smalley's 6000 series but neither was it a 5 series. A compromise was reached – it would be a Smalley 6005!

This little monster was returned to Cromford (*above*) in the mid -1980's. It had three huge rolling drums which gave floatation on water and movement on land (it was theoretically amphibious) and which could be hydraulically raised and lowered or swung in and out. The machine was remarkably stable and just what we needed.

70

A few years earlier we had acquired a redundant work punt, seen above and below, (from Wakefield Boat Co. again) which had been of great help along the canal. It was unpowered and was christened *Blue Streak* as without help it was going nowhere. For a short time it even carried the long reach machine as a bizarre Heath-Robinson dredger! A bonus from converting the original machine into a dredger was that its original engine was returned to us as redundant. Our naturalist friends frowned on anything with a propeller but had no objection to a paddle wheel, so the old engine was fitted to *Blue Streak*, a suitable hydraulic motor found and our workshops married these into a paddle wheel which was hung on the back of the punt. *Blue Streak* now had power! Immediately the boat became essential for moving up and down the canal, and was perfectly capable of pulling *John Gray* or the dredger from one place to another.

In the constant battle against leaks we started to use steel piling on some particularly vulnerable parts of the towpath. A number of areas just outside Cromford Wharf were tackled with a portable hydraulic generator connected to a hydraulic jackhammer. The jackhammer was sufficiently light to be handled by a couple of men and a special piling head (essentially a block of hardened steel on a shaft) allowed us to drive 6 ft interlocking piles into the banks.

With *Blue Streak* now in powered mode we added a hydraulic take-off to the system which then allowed us to transport the piles with ease and to work straight off the boat to insert them in the banks. These two pictures give a good indication of how the job was done, the piling head can be seen clearly.

Apart from the noise the only real problem was in the high tensile steel of the connecting shaft which had a tendency to shear off after a while. When this happened the whole assembly had to be taken back to the workshop, warmed up with a gas torch, and a new tapered shaft fitted. This happened quite often.

The operation shown here is of a small number of piles being inserted to protect a low and narrow section of towpath opposite Pisani's works, just north of Brown's Bridge.

Over the next year or so the new floating machine was able completely to dredge the main line between Cromford and Leawood. This was the first time the canal was properly cleared of obstruction by mud and weeds. It was particularly good to see the heavily blocked section at Pisani's wide and clear. By removing the old fixed bridge on Leawood Aqueduct we could move the dredger on to more serious work towards Gregory Tunnel. The Railway Aqueduct, having proper sets of stop planks at each end, could be used as a lock (*above*) to access the currently lower water level beyond. Then work could begin on the next section (*below*), already badly weeded even after dredging by the old Smith 14 (*see* pages 48 and 49).

With clearance completed on the section between railway Aqueduct and Gregory Nip it was clear that the whole length required extra protection. This was the section which had breached on 21 February 1920 and which still leaked (*see* p.21). The decision was taken with DCC to reinforce the whole section with steel piles. We had anticipated this when the 6005 was being built and specified a hydraulic take-off from its system so that external equipment could be used.

The first piles were inserted at the south end of Railway Aqueduct (*above and below*) in April 1988. The piles were brought down from Cromford in *Blue Streak* and landed at the aqueduct. Then as many as were needed were brought to the machine by dumper truck. The dredger also made a very good solid platform from which to work.

A considerable amount of work was done on this section until finally we could stop at Gregory Nip (*above*). The gap between piles and bank was back-filled with spoil as we moved along, thus helping to widen the towpath.

Below: The finished job, looking towards Railway Aqueduct. The dumper truck, bottom left, is just short of the original breach site.

Above: The 6005 working its way towards Gregory Tunnel. Spoil was unloaded into dumpers which then carried it away to tipping sites agreed with DCC and DNT.

Below: Just before the long straight to the tunnel. It was from this point that the Smith 14 had to be 'floated' for 150 yards. Running underneath the canal here is a small culvert which drains a stream from the hillside on the left. On the right a spillway had been installed beneath the towpath to help overflow in times of heavy rain.

Mindless vandalism was always a problem along the canal, but none more so than between the Railway Aqueduct and Gregory Tunnel.

Above: A window smashed on the 6005 in March 1988. *Below*: The same kind of attack on the Smith 14 in almost exactly the same place a decade earlier. The attack on the Smith was done with old spark plugs and a catapult. In both cases, valuable time was lost to make expensive repairs and steel shutters had to be added to prevent further damage. Trying to understand the mindset of people who do this kind of thing is soul destroying. It never failed to astound us that anyone should want to attack or to interfere with work which would ultimately benefit the local community.

Above: The 6005 at the culvert mentioned on p.76 after the canal has been cleared. The digger bucket is over a small "silt trap" constructed some years earlier. This is an excellent picture to show how the stabilisers on the pontoon are manipulated for stability.

Below: Approaching the 42 yard Gregory Tunnel in late April 1988.

For some reason stop plank grooves were never built into the ends of Gregory Tunnel. It was thought expedient that at least one end ought to be able to control water levels, especially as a reasonable amount of water was required back to Leawood but a lower level needed for dredging in Gregory Dam.

Above and right: Work in progress at the north end of the tunnel in May 1988 to install a proper sill and grooves for planks. Water was held back with (yet another) wiggly tin dam across the canal and a sludge pump kept proceedings reasonably dry. When the work was finished the dam was removed and the new stop planks could do a proper job of controlling water.

Gregory Tunnel following restoration. The new stop planks are just visible (*above*) at the mouth of the tunnel. The footpath over the top can be seen on the right of the picture. Whilst on this side the path is a fairly gentle slope up to a stile near the parapet wall, on the other side of the tunnel what path there is is near-vertical. The notion that horses would be uncoupled and led over the top is therefore difficult to believe, especially as there is a good fenced towpath right through the tunnel.

Below: The 6005 had to dig its way out of the tunnel due to debris in the canal.

Above: Gregory Dam as found.

Right: Gregory Dam during clearance in June 1988.

Cutting a winding hole into the vast reed beds choking Gregory Dam. Here the machine was in its element as (even though the level was low) the water was very deep. It could work well away from land without any problems, except coming back for a cup of tea.

Gregory 'Dam' (*below*) is an odd topographical feature. There is a depression in the land here, largely covered with a layer of boulder clay. It looks very like Jessop simply made an embankment on the lower side – on the right in the picture below – and more or less allowed the canal's water to find its own boundary on the gently sloping land to the left. As a result the Dam was formed as a useful turning place between Leawood and the next wide place between Gratton's Bridge and Poyser's Bridge. The monument of Crich Stand can be seen on top of the hill above the dredger.

Having cleared a winding hole near the tunnel entrance the 6005 could make its way towards Leashaw Bridge (Br 9) in June 1988.

Above: The machine working in the increasingly confined channel approaching Leashaw Bridge in July 1988. Considerable run-off from the fields above the canal on the right had left the canal almost completely filled with silt and gravel.

Below: The finished job at Leashaw looking rather more attractive than before. This was the farthest extent of dredging for the 6005 as it was required to do work further up the canal (*see* later) and in any case there would be difficulties in tackling the Leashaw-Robin Hood section which we had not yet solved.

With the line at least in partial water all the way from Leawood to the tunnel attention turned to controlling levels beyond Gregory Dam.

Some years earlier we had found another culvert running under the canal (to drain land above) about 200 yards north of Leashaw Bridge and opened part of its roof to allow drainage of the Dam. This now became the site of a new overflow. The culvert was repaired and modified (*left*) and a new brick structure added with a small sluice at its bottom and a set of short stop planks above. This allowed levels in that section to be raised or lowered according to requirements. (It is also visible in the lower picture on p.82.)

Even with the canal badly blocked past Leashaw, and the heavy wooden barrage at Robin Hood, a small amount of water could be diverted along the line to Whatstandwell where it could flow along the partially dredged channel to Ambergate. This was the first time a flow from Cromford to Ambergate had been realised.

The canal just after Robin Hood (*below left*), and through Sims Bridge (Br 12) (*below right*), displays at least some water flowing. It would have been an excellent prospect to restore this beautiful part of the canal but circumstances dictated otherwise.

The last remaining obstacle to navigation through the tunnel was the fixed bridge across Leawood Aqueduct. The original had replaced the long-gone swing bridge (Br 6) by way of a couple of steel joists filled with concrete. This was removed some years earlier and changed to a timber structure which was now 'lifted' on railway sleepers to allow enough room to squeeze *Blue Streak* underneath. (On occasion the whole bridge was floated out of the way on *Blue Streak* to get the dredger past.)

In October and November 1988 the last big project by our Job Creation Team was to re-create the swing bridge on its original site. The bridge was designed in steel by DCC and fabricated at Robinson's works at Longcliffe. It was galvanised and then the parts were delivered to Cromford Wharf. Meanwhile a completely new bearing pad was built on the site of the original bridge, its centre being carefully measured to take the new construction. The new steel beams were delivered to site by *Blue Streak* and bolted to the ball-race already installed (*above*) then the cross-braces and hand rails could be bolted on to those (*below*).

Temporary ballast was used (*above*) for a trial opening to check the swing and the structure could then receive a coat of bitumastic paint. The floor boards were bolted into place afterwards.

The bridge number no longer existed so we made a copy out of fibreglass similar to those on the aqueduct. *Below*: The finished bridge in 1991, (after CCS departed) no longer opening and with paint peeling.

21 December 1988 was the last working day of that year's Job Creation Team. It was arranged that *John Gray* would make the trip all the way from Cromford to Gregory Dam by way of celebration of their year's work and to test the line for navigation. (Whether they liked it or not!) *John Gray* was towed by *Blue Streak*, passing over Leawood Aqueduct and through Bridge 6 (*above*) and on to the Railway Aqueduct (*below*), then along the newly piled section to a sharp-ish corner at Gregory Nip. This would be the first test of the passenger boat through Gregory Tunnel.

Above: Entering Gregory Tunnel.

There were no serious problems and *John Gray* turned at the new winding hole in Gregory Dam before returning through the tunnel to pause for a break (*below*).

Then the return journey.

Above: Negotiating the Railway Aqueduct.

Below: Approaching Leawood. The swing bridge is open (not yet painted). The Nightingale Branch is on the right of this picture by the large tree.

Whilst in passing, wishing a Happy Christmas to the 6005 parked by the spillway at Leawood (*above*).

We did not know it at the time but this would be the first and last navigation by passenger boat between Cromford and Gregory Dam. In February 1989, sixty nine years to the month after the last major breach, the canal overtopped in two places between the Railway Aqueduct and Gregory Tunnel. The cause was exceptionally heavy rain falling on snow on the hills above Cromford. At the same time high winds brought down small branches which progressively blocked 3 spillways, causing exceptionally high water levels. The first damage was in exactly the same place as the 1920 breach (*below*). Only the piles installed a year before prevented a total disaster.

Two pictures of the overtopping in 1989:

Below left: 9 year old David Stoker looks at the damage on the morning immediately after the storm (the canal is being drained). *Below Right*: A little while later when DCC had put some fencing round the dangerous bit. The water level is now down to the minimum.

The second overtopping (*above*) between silt trap/culvert (p.78) and the tunnel was arguably far more dangerous. Here there were no steel piles to support the embankment, which itself was of quite soft and crumbly material. Although this embankment was by no means as tall as the breach site, it was probably much less stable and thus more vulnerable.

Some time later the site received a group of DCC officials to discuss the possibility of repairs (*below*). Various figures and ideas were mentioned at the time but nothing positive was achieved. Note that vegetation has had time to spring up since the damage occurred. After that stormy night the whole section south of Leawood was drained for safety and never regained a navigable condition. Passenger boats would never again operate here.

Despite the setbacks there was still a canal to run. 1989 was the first year in a decade that we had no Job Creation workforce to help with maintenance or restoration. Despite that boat trips were run and the beam engine was steamed on a regular basis. We were allowed the use of the larger warehouse at Cromford Wharf, and by July 1989 part of the middle floor was converted for an information point and shop.

Above: Gary and Dennis Shooter (son and father), the other two CCS employees, who did much of the work in converting the available space. The shop counter was designed as a replica of *John Gray* and there was plenty of space for meetings. It proved quite successful.

Motive Power

(About a horse)

It is a common misconception that to pull a narrowboat you need an animal the size of a small house, like a Clydesdale. In fact the latter would be too big for most bridge holes and too heavy because it would have to 'check' its weight against the towline all the time. Historically many boats used elderly Hansom Cab horses or similar animals. On land one horse can pull about one ton, on rails it can pull about three tons. On water it can pull up to thirty tons.

Over the years we had a number of horses of varying ages, mainly lent to us by kind owners. They were not worked hard and on some occasions we had more than one horse available for work.

Above left: 'Major' one of our earlier animals.

Above right: 'Strawberry' (Left) and 'Pie' (Right), always a favourite with schools visitors. 'Strawberry' was a former pit pony living out his days with a local family who generously allowed us to make use of his services.

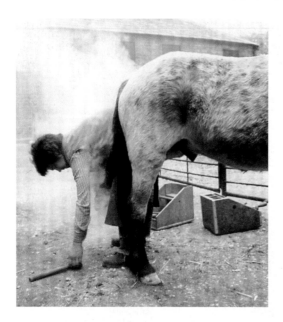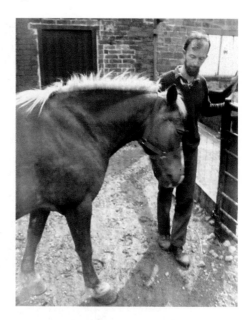

The animals had to be fed hay and pony nuts because there was little available non-toxic grass nearby.

Above left: The smoke is entirely due to the horse being re-shod (which was a regular event) and not the feed.

Above right: A large Haflinger mare lent to us for a season by the Duchess of Devonshire. The Duchess was a well known breeder of Haflingers on the Chatsworth Estate where they were used in their traditional role as forestry horses. This animal weighed the best part of a ton and on her first trip with the boat treated it as a large log being pulled out of a forest. She would happily have pulled it along the towpath (probably without noticing) until trained to take things rather more gently.

It was not unusual to find people on the towpath with no concept of just how a horse pulls a boat (it leans on the towline to start with and then just has to keep a gentle pace for the moving boat to follow).

On one occasion we were repeatedly hailed from the towpath all the way from Brown's Bridge to Cromford by a lady who had decided that any animal doing work should be banned immediately! Despite it being explained to her that she was looking at one of the oldest forms of commercial transport and that the animal was not in distress she refused to be cowed.

There were regular complaints from the "Horse and Pony Protection Society" (or some such name) who no doubt do very good work elsewhere. As a result there were regular visits from the RSPCA until an Inspector turned up and told us: "I could see there was nothing wrong with that animal from 100 yards away." It may be that after that the RSPCA had words with the complainers, for we rarely saw them again. After all, who is going to abuse their bread and butter?

ADS

Above: Horse maintenance on Cromford Wharf.

Right: 'Tina'. This mare was the first (and only) horse actually purchased by CCS. She was a thoroughbred Haflinger, although not from the Duchess' stable. (Her proper name was Edial Christina II). Weighing about half a ton she was ideal for boat work – not too heavy or bulky, and slightly shorter than some of her predecessors. Of Austrian descent she could be awkward when a mood took her, but we thought of her mainly as a big blonde bossy hausfrau. She was certainly the most attractive of all the horses we used and much admired on working days.

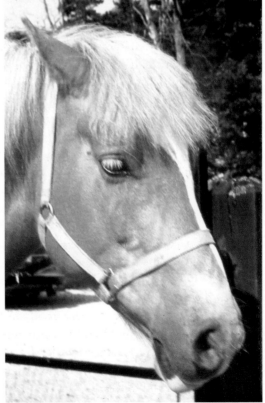

Right: 'Tina' fully dressed for work. The harness was fairly simple, being essentially two ropes (with bobbins to prevent rubbing) attached to the collar and running to a swingletree behind. All the load was taken by the collar onto the horse's shoulders, her strongest part. The hames round the collar, to which the ropes attached, were specially made so that the usual curled and decorative tops were altered so as not to foul under bridges. The back and belly straps are to prevent the bobbins from riding up or down.

One event in 1986 became the subject of minor legend. It happened that the sitting MP for West Derbyshire had decided to quit and therefore a by-election was called. One of the political parties involved thought it would be a useful stunt to involve the *John Gray* and the Press. (No bother to us and the fee was useful.) Accordingly a rather nervous prospective MP and various minders arrived at Cromford Wharf where they would take a trip along the canal and answer Press questions along the way. Mrs Thatcher was probably at the peak of her tenure in Downing Street and for some reason the by-election attracted more than usual attention. Fleet Street's finest (including the late Vincent Hannah, various well-known broadsheet hacks and a camera crew) assembled on board *John Gray* to be offered quantities of Desmond Stoker's home made sherry (which they did not refuse, even though it was heavily fortified with brandy!). *John Gray* set off towards Leawood and the assembled hacks fired questions at the prospective MP as arranged. After half a mile or so the reporters ran out of questions. What they had not realised was that *they could not get off the boat* until we stopped at Leawood, being rather more used to rushing off to file their copy from the nearest hostelry. A dozen of Britain's best reporters twiddled thumbs in embarrassed silence and did not seem at all interested in the canal – not their thing after all – until one turned to the steerer and asked the name of the horse. "Tina", came the honest reply, whereupon assorted hacks burst into gales of laughter. They had a story! We were exceeding puzzled that a horse's name should provoke such hilarity. Arriving at Leawood the reporters vanished into thin air and we were left with the candidate and his minders who were asked why such mirth at the horse's name. The rather peeved reply was; "It's an acronym of Mrs Thatcher's mantra, *There Is No Alternative*".

The next day the *Guardian*, *Observer* and others all ran amusing stories based on TINA. The candidate was elected with a slim majority of 100 and is now Chief Whip for his Party and a Privy Councillor.

Extras

In twenty years of working on the Cromford Canal there were times when the unusual was quite welcome.

Above left: An abandoned duckling rescued on Cromford Wharf. Despite what some lurid headlines in the local press might have implied there was always considerable thought for the flora and fauna of the canal. Indeed, the near-stagnant bog we had approached in 1968 became, after restoration, a haven for a wide variety of bird life, including Kingfishers, Little Grebe, Moorhens and many more, something which embarrassed our detractors who predicted devastation down the Derwent Valley!

Moorhens are not the cleverest of creatures and build nests in the most unusual places.

Above right: This nest was nearly halfway across the canal, clinging to a few stalks of willow. In successive years a moorhen nested virtually overnight on the rear end of *Blue Streak*. Once on the paddle wheel cowling (*below right*) and later (*below left*) inside the paddle wheel itself! *Blue Streak* was thus out of action until the eggs hatched.

A spin-off from restoring the beam engine was that various people contacted us to say they had a steam engine of some kind needing a good home and would we look after it. We were given this massive Robey engine (*above and below*) by Derbyshire Silica Firebrick of Friden, near Buxton, on condition that it was restored and remained on exhibition in Derbyshire. The original plan was to house it on Cromford Wharf but this came to nothing, so a large tin shed on Cromford Meadows (next door to the wharf) was leased to house this and

other bits of machinery. It was a twin-cylinder Robey built in 1902 which originally supplied motive power to parts of the brickworks. Recovery was a nightmare as it was right inside the works, but it was brought to Cromford in pieces and over several years carefully restored.

The Steam Museum, as it came to be called, became an additional interest to visiting parties, particularly as it used considerably less coal than the Leawood Pump. Over time a significant collection of steam engines came to be housed in that shed, some on loan and some gifted to us. When regular Steam Rallies were held on Cromford Meadows our little museum helped remind people that there was a canal next door.

In addition to the use of the beam engine for a significant segment of one "Sources of Power" programme for the Open University, there were occasional visiting film crews for both BBC and ITV local news. As can be seen *above left*, East Midlands Today, filming a group of exchange students who took a trip on *John Gray*.

From time to time we were asked to provide the background to other events.

Above right: Two models pose on *John Gray* for a calendar shoot arranged by Adshead Ratcliffe, a local company who became great friends and gave us generous financial help. Perhaps the canal's biggest opportunity came early in 1985 when we were asked to provide a location for a BBC crew filming Silas Marner, with (now Sir) Ben Kingsley in the title role. *John Gray* was disguised to look like a broken down narrowboat and filming took place around Lawn Bridge.

Below left: Ben Kingsley discussing his motivation. *Below Right:* Crew and two CCS 'extras' with 'Strawberry' awaiting the first take.

To film one man for a short sequence took more than 30 people, several vans and a catering bus, two deep freeze trailers, make-up vans and the camerman's vehicle. It took all morning to get ready when the union called for a lunch break. Immediately 30 people plus two extras queued at the catering van for their meal. Ben Kingsley was last in the queue. When asked why he was last and not first he replied: "I'm only the f******g actor!"

Above left: John Gray at Lawn Bridge with two of our Job Creation Team waiting for instructions. The boat was manhandled backwards from the wharf and for about 100 yards past the bridge. On "Action" we needed several strong men to push the boat to mid-canal so that little 'Strawberry' had a chance of taking the load. Ben Kingsley is in the foreground.

Above right: The disguised stern of *John Gray*. Luckily we had a sign-writer on the Job Creation Team who produced a beautiful cabin sign for the occasion. It was an anagram of our names. In the background the camera crew occupy *Blue Streak* to get the right shot, exactly on the apex of the corner leaving Lawn Bridge where the stern of a narrowboat swings out! We warned them about this but they did not want to move and as a result nearly lost a very expensive Arriflex camera!

Below: Dennis Shooter and Simon Stoker, with 'Strawberry', dressed as extras. We did not argue with the Costume Department's idea of what boatmen looked like! The Equity rate for non-speaking extras was at that time £34.50 a day. Meg, the dog we carried on the roof (in the picture above), was worth £18 a day!

It took three quarters of a day for thirty plus people, one actor, one boat and a dog to film this sequence. When transmitted on 30th Dec 1985 we got 8½ seconds airtime! However, CCS earned a significant location fee, which made a valuable contribution to that year's income.

On 12 August 1988, his 79th birthday, Desmond Stoker made a sponsored bow-haul of *John Gray* from Leawood to Cromford Wharf. He raised over £1,000, at the same time proving to some critics that if a horse does not actually have to do much once it has started a boat moving then neither did he.

Above: Crossing Brown's Bridge with boat in tow. *Below:* Assembled members of the local press photograph his arrival at Cromford.

End of the Line

Above: John Gray abandoned and unloved straddling the stop planks of the dry dock at Cromford after CCS went out of business. She was later sold off and is now on the Thames with an awful 'conversion' for living accommodation.

. . . And Back Again

Epilogue

The Cromford Canal Society Ltd ceased to exist in 1990. Twenty years on – nearly a generation – to visit the canal in the knowledge that it could be (and has been) so much more is perhaps disturbing and depressing. The pictures which follow are the result of visits to the canal – the same kind of visit which might be made by any tourist – and the comments here relate to what was seen at the time. Of course, there are times when the canal is more popular and there is more activity, but this is what was seen then.

On the surface Cromford Wharf looks nice enough. The area has been 'prettyfied' and tidied. But it is empty. There is not much to say what went on here. Nothing much about which canal it is and where it goes. Cromford Wharf (*above*) is almost sterile. It looks well enough. A tranquil scene one late May morning in 2008. Ducks quack in the distance somewhere, a few people walk their dogs along the towpath, three cars and a caravan are parked in the (now Pay and Display) car park. Very quiet. Look again. This could be a not very well maintained corporation pond or a half-forgotten municipal park. How many people now realise it is the terminal wharf of a once-busy canal? The main (peninsular) wharf is devoid of feature; a grassy, slightly lumpy, piece of ground on the other side from the car park with no identifying features. What there is now is still much appreciated by those who love a quiet place or a gentle walk, and in that there is no criticism. When this picture was taken the area had received 2½ inches of rain in three days so there was ample water in the canal. Looking at the channel it is not difficult to see that the bottom is very near the top. A lack of moving boats and an absence of dredging is fast producing the very same conditions found in 1968. Pretty it may be. Quiet it is. A canal . . .?

The 15 miles of Derwent Valley south of Matlock was listed as a World Heritage Site on 16th December 2001. Thus it is of the same importance as (say) the Pyramids, Stonehenge or the Jurassic Coast of Devon. (Of the currently 788 WH Sites listed in 2004, 27 are in the UK.) Of course the listing was largely due to the concentration of mills along the valley. Part of the local website records; *". . .Arkwright sought a reliable source of water but he was also attracted by the easy availability of child labour in and around Cromford, where the lead mining industry offered little scope for the employment of young children."*

(Derwent Valley Mills-World Heritage Site).

The feeder from the mill (*right*) is now overgrown. With the removal of the concrete measuring weir the bypass channel constructed in 1979 is redundant. It is still there behind the clumps of ferns but no longer used. It is not possible to inspect the inflow from the culvert due to heavy overgrowth.

The restored feed of 'warm' fresh water (*below right*) has been abandoned and its outlet is choked with reeds. Does nobody have the time to clear a 10 ft by 6 ft rectangle?

Behind the culvert, the stable built for CCS horses, has been removed, which at least gives a very clear indication of the line of the culvert and the odd shape of the office. The heavy wooden shutters on the office building have not been painted since CCS departed. A man was there pottering about at the office. He did not know what bitumastic paint was, or why the shutters had not been painted for 20 years, or even what shutters were.

The canopy on the larger warehouse is intact (*above*), although the building itself looks closed up and unused. The loading dock is heavily fouled with blanket weed, another result of poor water flow without the feed culvert at the right hand end of the canopy. The smaller warehouse (*below*) is in use. It is now a Tea Shoppe (or something), as evidenced by the picnic tables outside. At least the crane, re-created with such care in that very building, when it was properly used as a workshop, is still visible by the drydock. There is no external interpretation of this building, so visitors might wonder what it was.

Few would recognise the only feature on the far side of the wharf – a heap of scrap (*above*). In fact this scrap is the remains of two important artifacts: the wrought-iron ribs of the icebreaker rescued from Leawood (its timbers long gone), and, more importantly, the broken up remains of the cast iron footbridge (a Scheduled Monument) rescued from Bull Bridge Aqueduct. It was to be repaired and exhibited at the Wharf, its base stone is still visible by the feeder culvert on p.104. Along the towpath some work has taken place to remove reeds. The stems still in place towards the middle of the channel (*below*) show how far the channel had been choked.

The trees are back (*above*) around Lawn Bridge and the first few yards of canal after that look quite clear (allowing for the shallow water). Walk up to the top of the bridge (*below*) and look towards Leawood and it becomes clear that the reeds are busy making their way across the channel again.

The volunteer effort in removing these pernicious and aggressive water plants is commendable but the owners of the canal should not rely on a few weekend working parties. It needs regular and proper maintenance.

Further along, near Pisani's (*above*) the scale of overgrowth, undergrowth and weed growth becomes much more apparent. Blanket weed is choking the canal, depriving both creatures and other plants of sunlight and oxygen. Blanket weed *never* appeared with the canal in operation.

The approach to Brown's Bridge (*below*) is in similar condition. At least the towpath is clear.

Brown's Bridge (*above*) is in poor condition and showing an appalling lack of maintenance. The timbers are suffering and the (replacement steel) rails have not seen paint for many years. Just how long does it take to give it a coat of black and white? A ranger at the High Peak visitor centre did not know but said something about Risk Assessments. This bridge is possibly the most well used on the upper part of the canal and is the first thing many visitors see when they come to view the railway. Surely an image of decay should be the last thing to impress visitors?

At High Peak Wharf (*right*) the blanket weed is as thick as ever. *Duchess* and *Blue Streak* languish alongside the Wharf Shed.

High Peak Wharf (*right*) in late May 2008. *Duchess* and *Blue Streak* are moored out of the way and a little aluminium punt is chained to the cast iron stanchions. It should be noted that there are a number of interpretation boards around the High Peak section which give a fair explanation of current work.

The welcome at the railway sheds at the bottom of the Sheep Pasture incline is always warm and the exhibits there are worth seeing.

Looking towards Leawood Aqueduct from the same position (*below*) gives an impression of the 'country park' thinking involved. It may be pretty but it is not correct! The tree growing out of the coping stones has in the past caused damage and is doing so again. Ivy grows up the poles supporting an electricity transformer which supplies the pumphouse. Blanket weed is everywhere.

The winding hole at Leawood (*above*) has undergone some fairly heavy tree clearance and (again) it looks very pretty. This is, however, something of an illusion in the manner of a country park rather than a working (or not) canal. Looking closer it is impossible to disguise the rot and the lack of paint showing on the oak railings surrounding the pump output pipe (*below*) – *see* pages 43 and 44.

The aqueduct at Leawood (*above*). The oak baulks installed to protect the Schlegel Membrane (installed at a cost in excess of £20,000 to stop leakage) are growing some healthy weeds and some are missing. Bridge 6 (*below*) at the end of the aqueduct has not moved for a very long time. The water level past the stop planks is about a foot lower than that in the aqueduct.

Aqueduct Cottage (*above*) is almost completely obscured by tree growth, as is the entrance to the Nightingale Branch. Meanwhile the 'country park' appearance seems to dissipate after Leawood and the canal is badly overgrown (*below*). The towpath is unsurfaced and at times very muddy.

Railway Aqueduct (*above*) is also badly overgrown. There are no stop planks in position at either end. Previous experience would suggest one set should be available as a precaution. Where the canal overtopped in 1989 (*below*) the towpath has simply been fenced to prevent visitors falling down the embankment. Whilst the surface has been stabilised the embankment still bears the scars of the washout twenty years before. No reinforcement has been done, although trees and scrub grow where water washed away the side. (*See* picture p.90).

Gregory Tunnel is similarly in urgent need of attention. Both the north (*above*) and south (*below*) portals are heavily overgrown which cannot be doing the stonework much good.

The southern end of the tunnel (*above*) is almost completely obscured, although Gregory Dam (*below*) is sufficiently clear of reeds to show its purpose on the canal.

Above: The view from Leashaw Bridge (Br 9) looking towards Gregory Dam. This photograph was taken from the same position as the ones on p.83. Again silt has been washed into the narrow channel (bottom right in the picture and the cause of the brown discolouration) from the steep hillside above and there is little room for water.

Below: Leashaw Bridge, looking towards Robin Hood. The stop planks are still in place, although after heavy rain they are allowing a small flow of water towards Whatstandwell. There is a 270 ft OS Benchmark on the stonework (*inset bottom right*). The normal water level would have been about 3ft below this mark, making the contour approximately 267 ft.

The section from Leawood to Whatstandwell is arguably one of the most beautiful lengths of canal anywhere in England.

Above: The delightful cottage at Robin Hood, now in excellent condition, on the sharp right-hand bend towards Whatstandwell. The heavy baulks of timber (foreground) inserted across the canal after its serious leak have now become a permanent walkway for the owner.

Left: What came to be known as the 'Davis Foundry' section, about 100 yards re-puddled by DCC and now in water. At the time of photographing there was a welcome flow of water towards Whatstandwell, although given the number of silt deltas across the channel this may well have been because of run-off from recent heavy rain.

Above: Sims Bridge (Br 12) looking towards the 'Davis' section. The original girder structure, which carried the tramway down from Duke's Quarries, was replaced by DCC with a light steel version.

Below: The approach to Whatstandwell Bridge (Br 13). The bottom left of this picture gives a clear indication of how little water is actually in the channel. There was always a problem along this section caused by slippage from the steep and unstable bank on the offside of the canal, as can be seen by the bulges in the reeds on the left.

Above: The southern side of Whatstandwell Bridge, as usual showing comprehensive blockage. Drainage is being piped from near the road.

Right: From Whatstandwell Bridge looking towards Crich Chase.

Above left: Hays Wharf and the Red Cross Cottages.

Above right: Grattons Bridge (Br 15) looking towards Ambergate. In both these pictures the skeleton of an old maintenance flat boat can be seen under the trees, where it has been for very many years.

Below: The winding hole 100 yards south of Grattons Bridge. This may look an idyllic picture, and it can be seen that some weed clearance has taken place. However, in places the water is only inches deep. A number of field drains between this point and the terminus have deposited silt in banks right across the channel which, in times of dry weather, will impede water flow and cause stagnation.

Above: Leading up to Poysers Bridge (Br 16) the channel is almost completely blocked by silt from field drains (a lovely medium for reed growth). In one place there is less than an inch of water, even after heavy rain.

Below: Looking through Poysers Bridge towards the terminus at Ambergate. Without urgent work the future of this part of the canal is as dark as the bridge hole.

Locked Pounds

At the time of writing, Derbyshire County Council is to receive a substantial grant from the East Midlands Development Council of something approaching £600,000 over three years. Naturally, in the first instance, it was necessary to conduct a thorough survey of the 5 miles between Cromford and Ambergate. To the surprise of some – but not to navigators – the consultants concerned recommended (among other things)[1]:

A 4 m wide by 90 cm deep channel (13 ft x 3 ft) *along the whole length of the canal* to accommodate trip and maintenance boats.
Reinforce the appearance of the canal as an engineered waterway.(!)
Prepare a phased dredging programme.
Repair and clear wharf edges.
De-vegetate and repair canal structures.
Provide additional manpower to maintain the canal.
Acquire appropriate maintenance plant and equipment.

There is an element of *deja vu* in all this. It is surely to be welcomed that professional consultants have come up with plans nearly identical to those promulgated and executed by CCS more than thirty years ago (and at virtually no cost). Perhaps if those responsible had been able to appreciate just what a bargain they had with CCS, the canal would not now look as it does in the preceding pages.

By way of example, when CCS made the decision to go full-time on the canal (and allowing for the additional input of Job Creation labour) it was arranged that DCC would award a grant-in-aid to cover maintenance costs on its property. In 1979 this amounted to £9,147.[2] In 1988, ten years later, the sum was £10,550.[2] In other words over that period the grant increased by just £1,403. However, inflation during that period was rampant, varying between 18% and 3.4%, so converting the above figures to 2007 values[3] they appear as £33,345 in 1979 but only £20,390 in 1988 – a reduction of nearly £13,000! Meanwhile over the same period CCS overheads went from £7,500 to £21,500 – a rise of 186%.

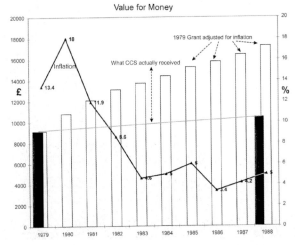

Value for Money

How times change.

Left: The first and last grants from DCC, as opposed to what they really ought to have been just to keep place with inflation. Given what was achieved the County Council got pretty good value for the ratepayers' money.

1 'Cromford Canal Conservation Management Plan 2007' - DCC web site.
2 Figures taken from CCS audited accounts, financial year Jan-Dec.
3 Conversions based on RPI from website www.measuringworth.com.

In fact, simply to keep up with inflation, the grant-in-aid should have been in the region of £17,300. The original concept of tourist income offsetting a diminishing grant from DCC could never be realised as inflation could not be predicted and was never factored into the calculations.

It is not difficult to see that CCS was badly short of funding during that period, using its own income to fund work on a public property. Reversing the calculations shown, the £600,000 quoted would be the equivalent of £310,500 in 1988. That would have made quite a difference to both the DCC and CCS budgets at the time, but the canal was not then part of a World Heritage Site and the EMDA did not exist. However, Leawood and Railway Aqueducts were always Scheduled Monuments and the Pumphouse was Grade II* listed and in the intervening twenty years more work should have been done to preserve them. The Pumphouse has recently undergone a partial roof replacement (for exactly the same reasons as 1973/4!) but the aqueducts need much more work. Now, of course, it is noted that the canal is a *"significant component of the Derwent Valley Mills World Heritage Site and the only canal in a UK WHS"* (DCC Website).

Significantly three of the bridges are now Grade II Listed and all three buildings at Cromford Wharf have been given the same status. (When CCS asked the County to list the wharf buildings this was refused because *"the buildings are not threatened"*. What has changed?) It is envisaged that the 2007 Management Plan will last for 20 years, with annual monitoring and quinquennial reviews.

All but 547 yards (500 m) of the Ambergate end of the canal is within the World Heritage Site (the odd bit being in a 'buffer zone', whatever that is). The lower section from Whatstandwell to Ambergate is a designated nature reserve and is managed by the Derbyshire Wildlife Trust (formerly the DNT). The whole canal was designated a Site of Special Scientific Interest in 1981, so the Trust has always had an interest in its operation, although the Trust records that it has 42 reserves in Derbsyhire (DWT web site).

Therein lies the same dichotomy: the demands of one organisation may not always coincide with another. In this case the Management Plan makes a strong case for a proper channel all the way to Ambergate, and from a canal point of view this makes considerable sense. It may not, however, make sense to those whose priority might be towards pond life. In other parts of the UK canal owners have come under considerable pressure from the naturalist lobby, to the extent where some restoration has gone to great lengths to accommodate demands. Getting the balance right will always be of major importance.

In the final analysis a canal is a man-made structure which requires continuous, sometimes critical, and often expensive maintenance. It is organic in that it bears no relation to modern concrete carbuncles but is more often made of local materials which, after 200 years, blend into its local environment as if they were a natural feature of the landscape. But it is not – a fact which must never be forgotten for that same canal will fight back if misused or allowed to decay. It cannot be frozen in time for the benefit of tourists, naturalists, engineers or any other group (connected or otherwise), and trying to destroy it will bring greater problems than keeping it alive. It can, with care and sympathy towards its special circumstances, be nurtured and brought into our 21st Century world for the benefit and education of a great many people, young and old alike. You can't kill a canal.

Midland Railway

Regular Staff employed on <u>Cromford Canal</u> + paid by the Engineering Dep.

No. of men	Grade	Present rate per day	Amount per week £ . s . d	Description of work
1	Canal Inspr	-	1 . 16 . 0	Supervision
1	Ganger	3/6	1 . 1 . 0	Repairs to towing path &c
1	,,-	3/8	1 . 2 . 0	
10	Labourers	2/10	8 . 10 . 0	
2	Gangers	4/-	2 . 8 . 0	Extra work, Dredging &c
3	Labourers	3/4	3 . 0 . 0	
1	Bricklayer	5/-	1 . 10 . 0	Repairs to Brickwork &c
1	Labourer	2/10	17 . 0	
1	Lock keeper	2/10	17 . 0	Repairs to Tools &c
1	Carpenter	4/6	1 . 7 . 0	
22			£ 22 . 8 . 0 = £1165 per annum	

A reproduction of one page of the notes supplied by Midland Railway (who owned the canal at that time) to the Royal Commission on Canals and Inland Waterways in 1908. The Canal Inspector is, of course, the most important and his wage translates to about £140 a week today. Unsurprisingly the Brickie, with his skill, is next on about £120 a week today. (No carpenter is mentioned.) The poor lock keeper would only be paid around £66.

*Conversions made using www.measuringworth.com, which uses the Retail Price Index and is not necessarily an absolute indication of modern values.

Information

The canal is still owned by Derbyshire County Council and enquiries may be made to:-

Countryside Services
Middleton Top Visitor Centre
Rise End,
Middleton by Wirksworth,
Matlock,
Derbyshire.
DE4 4LS
01629 823204
Or visit: www.derbyshire.gov.uk/leisure/countryside

Leawood Pumphouse
(and the Middleton Top Engine)

A small group has continued to operate the beam engine at Leawood on regular occasions.

There is now a link with the old railway incline winding engine at Middleton Top and information on both these engines can be found at: www.middleton-leawood.org.uk

FCC
Friends of the Cromford Canal

"The Friends of the Cromford Canal was formed in March 2002 to campaign for the restoration of the whole of the Cromford Canal from Langley Mill to Cromford including the Pinxton Arm. The FCC is keenly aware of the debt they owe previous restoration efforts. Without the hard work and dedication of the Cromford Canal Society on the Ambergate to Cromford section the task, although daunting, would be immeasurably more difficult, if not prohibitive. It is a sad fact that many of the CCS's efforts towards navigation are now lost under nearly twenty years of benign neglect. The FCC also owes a similar debt of gratitude to the Erewash Canal Preservation & Development Association; were it not for their efforts there would have been little to connect to at the Langley Mill end of the Cromford Canal. The Cromford Canal is just over 14 miles long in total and the FCC workload on the 5 miles from Ambergate to Cromford and at Langley Mill is less onerous as a consequence of past restoration efforts. Now for the (considerable) bit in the middle! If you are interested in the continuing battle to save the Cromford Canal please view our website www.cromfordcanal.org.uk.

Times have changed, but the aims remain the same: to see the Cromford Canal supporting what it was built for – boat traffic."

Patrick Morriss.
Chair, Friends of the Cromford Canal.

Index

Precious. So are canals.